Alain is especially gifted with a mind. This balance gives him the ability to lead us in an apostolic journey that's both biblically safe and Holy Spirit-empowered. His capacity to see much about the apostolic call and say it simply and practically makes this a rich read. Enjoy these pages that are filled with mature experience and a touch of the Spirit of revelation.

Doug Schneider

Apostolic leader, The Embassy of God
Toronto, Canada

The church is in a major shift, and a kingdom mindset with progressive vision is greatly needed. Alain Caron fills in the gaps for us in this season of changing garments with practical insights from his life's experience. Caron does an insightful job of developing new wineskin strategies for the day we live in.

Dr. James W. Goll

Encounters Network
Best-selling author

Alain Caron has written a book that builds bridges. As an apostolic leader of a local assembly of believers, he is uniquely positioned to write this practical blueprint that both inspires and instructs others on the process of transitioning local churches into apostolic centers.

Mark W. Pfeifer

Soma Family of Ministries
Chillicothe, Ohio

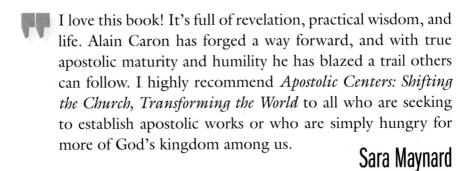

I love this book! It's full of revelation, practical wisdom, and life. Alain Caron has forged a way forward, and with true apostolic maturity and humility he has blazed a trail others can follow. I highly recommend *Apostolic Centers: Shifting the Church, Transforming the World* to all who are seeking to establish apostolic works or who are simply hungry for more of God's kingdom among us.

Sara Maynard
Founder/director Redleaf Prayer Ministries
Red Leaf House of Prayer
Ears2Hear Intercessory Network

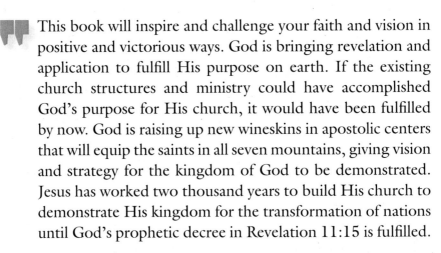

This book will inspire and challenge your faith and vision in positive and victorious ways. God is bringing revelation and application to fulfill His purpose on earth. If the existing church structures and ministry could have accomplished God's purpose for His church, it would have been fulfilled by now. God is raising up new wineskins in apostolic centers that will equip the saints in all seven mountains, giving vision and strategy for the kingdom of God to be demonstrated. Jesus has worked two thousand years to build His church to demonstrate His kingdom for the transformation of nations until God's prophetic decree in Revelation 11:15 is fulfilled.

Dr. Bill Hamon
Bishop, Christian International Ministries Network (CIMN)
Christian International Apostolic Network (CIAN)
Best-selling author

The restoration of apostolic centers is at the cutting edge of Holy Spirit's work in the church today. I see it shifting the New Apostolic Reformation to the next level and laying the groundwork for rapid territorial transformation. In *Apostolic Centers,* Alain Caron not only explains what this movement is about but provides a detailed case study of a traditional local church that successfully made the shift. I highly recommend this book for every Christian leader!

Dr. Robert Heidler
Apostolic teacher
The Global Spheres Center
Corinth, Texas

According to Dr. Paul Kennedy of Yale University, the world is experiencing monumental changes, the likes of which have not been seen for 500 years. Hence, the great need for a new wineskin in the church. It is no longer business as usual. We must look forward and prepare God's people to lead in a changing world. Alain Caron's timely book gives us a blueprint for such a time as this. Every pastor needs to read it and implement its wisdom in order to be relevant in these extraordinary times.

Wesley and Stacey Campbell
www.newlife.bc.ca
www.beahero.org
www.revivalnow.com

In the Book of Genesis, the first mention of the Holy Spirit is that He moved—and that gives us deep understanding of the very nature of God Himself. He moved in the beginning, He has moved in sequential waves of emphasis in past church history, and He is moving today! That means He will surely help motivate and move upon us as individual believers and as the corporate Body of Christ into His divine purposes for our generation and beyond.

Alain Caron unveils the revelation on the present movement of God through his successful life experience transitioning his own spiritual house from a traditional local church to an apostolic center. May the power of the *rhema* word contained herein stir up within your being and create a passionate desire to see Christ's government structure for His church.

Fernando Guillen
Chancellor, Wagner Leadership Institute in Brazil

 There has been a great shift in the administration of the church over the past twelve years, with an acceleration in the last three years. The Spirit of God is moving us from a "church" mentality into kingdom advancement. Jesus said to John's disciples in Matthew 11:11–12, "Assuredly, I say to you, among those born of women there has not risen one greater than John the Baptist; but he who is least in the kingdom of heaven is greater than he. And from the days of John the Baptist until now, the kingdom of heaven suffers violence, and the violent take it by force" (NKJV).

All kingdoms respond to a kingship. All kingdoms have a culture. All kingdoms have a language. But when you study the historical concept of kingdoms, they also have key places where their government, culture, and power are all demonstrated. In modern days, these places are called apostolic centers. At the end of May 2008, God showed me these centers forming. The driving force of each center was the glory of God.

Alain Caron has written a wonderful book called *Apostolic Centers: Shifting the Church, Transforming the World*. Not only does he communicate his own journey into apostolic rule, but also he discusses the apostolic mandate that was given to Jesus, our apostle. This apostolic mandate is supported by teams and networks and has a great sending power to cover the earth with the glory that is being sent from the apostolic center. One incredible chapter in this book is "How to Switch Wineskins without Spilling!"—in which Alain assesses how to shift wineskins from church to apostolic center without becoming torn in the process and spilling the new revelation for the future.

I have been privileged to visit Le Chemin in Gatineau, Quebec, across the river from Ottawa, Canada. What is written in this book is a reality. *Apostolic Centers* is a must-read for those in the process of making the shift from church to apostolic center in their ministry. I recommend this book for any leader who desires to hear what the Spirit of God is saying to the church at this time.

Chuck D. Pierce
President, Global Spheres Inc.
Glory of Zion Intl.

Alain Caron is one of those few leaders who has truly captured the pulse of what God is doing in our nation. Years of national ministry come to life with humility, wisdom, and application that make this book both enjoyable and a must-read on the subject of apostolic ministry.

Rob Parker

Founding director, National House of Prayer

As a prominent leader of the apostolic movement, Alain Caron is at the forefront of a revolution sweeping through the body of Christ. This book provides an honest account of his transitional journey and describes a fresh road map to instill groundbreaking change for the twenty-first century church. It is a fresh concept—rooted in ancient history and in God Himself—for authentic community that redefines the very nature of the church as a living organism rather than organization.

Danyele Bloom Holtner

National president, Aglow International Canada

APOSTOLIC CENTERS

SHIFTING THE CHURCH, TRANSFORMING THE WORLD

ALAIN CARON

HODOS
APOSTOLIC NETWORK

Published by Hodos
480 Vernon
Gatineau, Quebec J9J 3K5
Canada
(819) 778-2681
www.hodos.ca

ISBN: 978-0-9822653-3-8 (print)
ISBN: 978-0-9822653-4-5 (digital)

Cover and interior design: Rob Huff, ImageStudios
www.imagestudios.net

Edited by Amy Calkins, Aurora Writing and Editing Services
www.aurora-pub.com

13 14 15 16 17 18 19   7 6 5 4 3 2 1

DEDICATION

To Pastors Jean-Claude and Valerie Joyal, founders
of Le Chemin and true apostles who blazed the way.

To Duane and Connie MacMillan,
who believed in us from day one.

ACKNOWLEDGMENTS

I want to thank my dear wife, Marie, for her unfailing support and patience throughout the long hours of seclusion I took to write this book. Love you always, my sweet one.

A very big thank you to Diana Gumienny for all the reviews and corrections, the long hours, the short nights, and her commitment to excellence. Diana, you're the best.

A special thank you to Tim Knapp and Cory Gumienny for their valuable insight. You guys made me write a better book.

Thank you to my Le Chemin and Hodos families. Your prayers and your love mean a lot.

A warm thank you to C. Peter Wagner, who came into my life unexpectedly but at just the right time. You're a true dad.

A warm thank you to Doug Schneider for the inspiration he is to me. *Merci mon ami!*

Thank you to *Auntie* Pastor Sharon Rivest for her example of perseverance. If there was ever a woman apostle…

Thank you to David Demian, who mentored me in so many deep things in the heart of God. David, I'll always cherish those years spent with you.

CONTENTS

FOREWORD

by C. Peter Wagner

Apostolic Centers is a pioneer book for a new season of God's unfolding plan.

Let me explain what I mean.

Most Christian leaders—and many other Christians as well—understand that the personality of God is dynamic, not static. Although much of what God has revealed to us is permanent and unchangeable, the ways God chooses to carry out His purposes among us human beings are not. Look, for example, at the glimpse of God's character the prophet Daniel reveals to us: "Blessed be the name of God forever and ever, for wisdom and might are His. And He changes the times and the seasons..." (Dan. 2:20–21 NKJV).

Over my sixty years of ordained ministry, I have seen many of God's new seasons come upon the scene. In fact, for some of them, God has given me the privilege of being among the first to observe the new season and communicate it to leaders of the body of Christ. In doing this, I soon learned that each new season brings with it what Jesus called "new wine" (see Matt. 9:17). But Jesus also said God will pour His new wine only into new wineskins, not the old wineskins of the past season. In explaining this, Jesus was talking to disciples of John the Baptist, the last prominent representative of the season of the Old Covenant. Jesus and His disciples represented the new season of the New Covenant.

Jesus did not despise the old wineskin; in fact, He protected it. He knew that if new wine was poured into it, it would break, and He didn't want that. The old wineskin at one point in time was God's new wineskin. Jesus always honored John the Baptist. However, God is dynamic, not static. The New Covenant represented His plan for the future, and He was only going to pour new wine into New Covenant wineskins.

Over the years, I would have to say that the new season bringing the greatest magnitude of change that I have been able to observe has to do with the government of the church. Any casual reader of the New Testament would conclude that the governmental foundation of the church is apostles and prophets (see Eph. 2:20). Due to a combination of historical circumstances, the biblical government of the church largely went off the scene around three hundred years after the time of Jesus and the first apostles, and it did not reappear until relatively recent times.

Others may well see it differently, but my reading of history leads me to suppose that the new season began around 1900 with the African Independent Church Movement. It gained momentum with the emergence of the Chinese rural house church movement, the Latin American grassroots church movement, and the Independent Charismatic Movement in North America, all in the 1970s. Some call this new season the New Apostolic Reformation (NAR). It is bringing apostles back into church leadership, as Alain Caron vividly explains throughout this book.

Focusing for the moment on my home territory of North America, my best estimate is that the second apostolic age began here in 2001. That is when we reached a critical mass of churches moving into apostolic government, from which there will be no turning back. It is one of the current things the Spirit is saying to the churches.

All this is by way of background. Now to focus on this book,

Apostolic Centers. Since we have entered into the second apostolic age, God has begun to bring forth several additional new seasons. One of them is the phenomenon of certain traditional local churches transitioning into what are being called "apostolic centers." I have not seen any research that would tell us how many churches in North America have made this transition or are in the process. My guess is that it would be many hundreds and perhaps even move into the thousands. However, I feel certain that whatever the number, it is bound to increase in the years to come. It is a movement of the Holy Spirit that must not be ignored by church leaders.

I am personally acquainted with a number of pastors who have decided to make the transition. Most of them are planning on a slow, long-term process to get there from here. The major innovation is to switch from pastoral government to apostolic government. That means moving from the old wineskin of democratic church government, where the final authority is an elected board of elders or deacons or, in some cases, a vote of the entire congregation. The pastor serves at the pleasure of the decision-making group and, consequently, is an employee of the church. The new wineskin invests the final authority in the apostle. The apostle is no longer an employee but the equivalent of president and CEO.

You may have seen this before, but I am determined to repeat these two axioms on as many platforms as I possibly can until further notice. Why? I believe they form the heart of understanding the NAR and the second apostolic age:

- We are now witnessing the most radical shift in the way of doing church since the Protestant Reformation.
- Of all the changes, the most radical one is the delegation of authority by the Holy Spirit to individuals.

This, obviously, involves a paradigm shift that the majority of churches would not welcome. That is why, as you will see, Alain Caron carefully and consistently honors the many local churches

3

that will remain as local churches led by pastors, although he has some fine-tuning suggestions related to apostolic alignment.

What gives Alain Caron the credentials to write this book, possibly the first one on apostolic centers? His main credential is that he has done it. He has successfully transitioned a well-established traditional local church, Le Chemin, into a true apostolic center. He has supervised the change from the church being governed by a board of elders to which the pastor was accountable to one governed by an apostle supported by an apostolic council. Alain was the pastor; he is now the apostle.

Two additional things make Caron's transition even more remarkable:

- It was completed, from beginning to end, in only two years.
- Virtually no church members were lost in the process.

If you would like to know how such a thing was done, you will love this book. You will find solid biblical and theological foundations supporting the step-by-step process necessary to make it happen. It is truly a pioneer book for a new season!

C. Peter Wagner
Vice-President, Global Spheres, Inc.

PREFACE

The emergence of apostolic centers is the most radical shift coming to shake the global Christian world today. While the restoration of the apostles marked the first phase of the New Apostolic Reformation and produced all the ripples we know, the establishment of apostolic centers is about to become a tidal wave. This book is about that explosive transition.

In June 2012, I hosted a conference in Gatineau, Quebec, with C. Peter Wagner as the main speaker. As I was listening to him, I kept thinking about the key steps that can lead from new wineskins to social transformation. I had met Peter for the first time just the night before, and in our discussion, he had challenged me to write a vision statement that would reflect the practical metamorphosis we had undergone as a local church and the mandate I was receiving as an apostle. It came suddenly to me, early the following morning, prepackaged in a moment of revelation. Here it is:

> To activate the transformation of local churches into apostolic centers and link them into apostolic networks in order to establish alignment for territorial transformation.

In this book, I expand on the three components of this apostolic vision statement. I start with my own journey, and then I look at the apostolic mandate of the church, showing that from Jesus to

Paul, the same basic strategy has prevailed—an apostle surrounded by a team with a mission. Paul's journeys saw apostolic teams based in apostolic centers establish communities of believers everywhere, bringing transformation to the world, an original pattern that is being reactivated today.

Rediscovering the blueprint in Acts, we can see two types of governmental models emerging: the *pastoral church* and the *apostolic center*. We are familiar with the first; this is our traditional local church. The second model is the one rising up today.

The differences between the two are significant. To mention a few: While in a traditional local church, most of the activity is geared toward providing a safe environment to nurture the flock of God, in an apostolic center, the emphasis is on empowering the saints to release them into the harvest. The first can too often become maintenance oriented; the second thrives on development and expansion. The first can at times be quiet and unnoticed in the city; the second shakes the city.

But how can a local church become an apostolic center? Is this for all local churches? How long does it take?

A CASE STUDY

Our church is called Le Chemin (The Way). It is located in French Canada and successfully made the transition from a traditional local church to an apostolic center over a two-year period.

That transition involved both a reconfiguration of our view of the church and a reformatting of our government structure; we shifted from a board of elders to an apostolic team—a new structure for a new paradigm.

Switching wineskins is an interesting challenge, but with the right approach and the right process, it can be done without spilling a drop. I wanted to write a book that would not only give the theory but would also be a practical guide to help others in that transition. Not every local church will be called to become an apostolic center, but I believe everyone will be called to realign with the new configuration the Holy Spirit is bringing to the body of Christ.

When we started our two-year transition, we had about 150 people in our congregation; the Lord knew this was a size many churches would be able to relate to when they read our story. With that in mind, I followed the advice Doris Wagner gave me and wrote the book as a case study, featuring both Le Chemin and the early church of the Book of Acts.

You'll be able to follow the steps we made in order to transition well, but you'll also discover some of the key dynamics operating in our favor, like the law of apostolic attraction that activates team building. You'll see how redemptive alignment leads to governmental empowerment, and you'll read our own Adullam and Ziklag stories of alignments.

I also give numerous examples of the activation of the saints to exponential life, relating success stories of individuals, the expansion of the church, partnerships with business people, reproduction, and increased influence and authority in society, both locally and internationally.

The description of our Sunday celebration, in the chapter called "Party at the Gate" offers a compelling and inspiring picture to replace the old services many are used to.

LOOKING AHEAD

I've tried and tried but have never been able to change it; whenever I talk, preach, or write, I end up on the visionary side of things. Many Sundays I geared myself up to deliver a good pastoral message, only to end up launching vision before I finished speaking. I can't help it. That's who I am. This book is no exception.

In the last chapters, I look at how apostolic networks will link the apostolic centers and become a power grid for territorial governance. I believe they will be the most potent structure to support and sustain the end-time activation of kingdom dynamics. We are talking here of a transition from the old to the new, from legal structures to relational networks.

Finally, I envision a migration of apostolic teams from the mountain of religion to the other mountains of influence in society, establishing a new breed of apostolic centers. This will create new mountain ranges for a new spiritual landscape—a powerful geographical alignment able to produce territorial transformation.

This book is for all who hunger and thirst for a relevant church for the twenty-first century. It will be made up of pastoral churches and apostolic centers aligned with apostles and their teams. It will be empowered to impact and transform this world for kingdom establishment.

To the pastors who carry apostolic capacity and to the emergent apostles, this book will be a guide for the steps to transform local churches into apostolic centers. To the pastoral church leaders, it will be an encouragement to align apostolically. To the congregations, it will restore hope and excitement for the days we live in. Finally, for the seasoned apostles, visionary leaders, and deep thinkers, it will provide new tracks to explore.

The emergence of apostolic centers is not a wish. It's already a reality, and this spiritual movement is about to be activated to a whole new rate of expansion. We might only be at the pioneering stage, but the courageous outposts we are establishing are becoming the governmental headquarters for the kingdom of God. The earth is about to be transformed.

—Alain

PART 1

Transforming Local Churches into Apostolic Centers

CHAPTER 1

My Journey into the Apostolic

"Dad, do you ever wonder if God really exists?"

It was one of those warm summer nights at the cottage, and we were sitting on the wooden veranda, bare-chested, looking at the glittering of the moon on the lake. My dad bent forward and turned his head toward heaven. He was a strong man, larger than life, a Catholic free-thinker.

"Look at the sky," he said. "Do you see all those stars? Whenever I have doubts about God, that's what I do. I look at the stars, and I tell myself it's not possible they got up there by chance—there must be a Creator who placed them there."

I was just a boy, and I thought the world of my dad. The sky had never looked as majestic as it did that night, and from that point I was at peace with my existential questions—until my late teens. Then I lost my way.

LIVING MY LIFE

One thing my dad had produced in his sons was a strong adventurous spirit coupled with an enthusiasm to take the lead—a fine combination if you have honorable intentions, but not so good if you get mixed up with drugs.

I loved taking drugs with a passion—all kinds, all the time. Selling quickly became appealing, and I was probably the most joyful drug dealer in my city. It never stopped me from being involved in a multitude of ventures. I was a comedian, then a writer, then a producer in the theatre company at college—that was in the evenings. In the middle of the night, I printed communist propaganda. During the day, I attended meetings as a student council leader. Sleep? Didn't need much of that—too boring! Education? Well, I did two years in French literature, and then I went back later and did another two years in pure and applied sciences. I couldn't decide what end of the spectrum I wanted to stay on. I loved everything, which always included lots of drugs; I lived in the fading waves of the hippy era.

In 1979, I decided to explore the world with my girlfriend, my beautiful Marie, who would become my wife the following year. After four months of wandering through Europe, we ended up in Egypt, in January 1980. I'm glad there is a God who takes care of fools. We were traveling on cheap trains during the night, the kind of shady rides even Egyptians were telling us they wouldn't try; then we would meet and follow people we didn't know, finding ourselves in places way outside the regular tourist tracks, just having a great time.

Then one night something strange happened. We had met up with a friend from Canada a little while before, and we were travelling as a group of three. A guy we met brought us to a remote village, and when dusk fell, we found ourselves in a mud hut discussing religion with a group of Muslims. Soon, only the dim light of a few oil lamps allowed us to see the shadowed faces around us. We didn't know the men we were with, and the one who had brought us there had somehow disappeared.

The core of the discussion revolved around the existence of God. As young Canadian road trippers, we were making the point that the existence of God could not be proven. We had no problem with them believing there was a God, and we were totally ready to respect their right to have that belief, but the point remained that, if they wanted to be honest and admit it, nobody could prove God existed. The arguments went back and forth, and tension eventually filled the hut. Then one of them spoke with what I would call a sober authority and slowly said, "You are strangers here, and before you go farther in the conversation, I want you to know that in this country, if a man goes around saying he doesn't believe in God, that man can be killed at anytime." And he added, "As a friend, I just wanted to make sure you were aware of this."

At that moment, a tall and slim young man who was a student at the University of Cairo took me by the arm and said, "Come outside with me." I followed him.

If you have ever been in that part of the world, you have been conquered by the mysterious beauty of the desert continually crowned by the purest and most infinite sky that can exist. The display of glory above our heads that night was indescribable.

"Look at the sky," he said. "Look at all those magnificent stars. Can't you see there is one God who made all this?"

Something exploded inside of me. Broken segments of an old, forgotten pathway suddenly reconnected and brought me back to my roots, to the very faith of my father. My companion heard me say, my head turned to heaven, "Yes, I see it now. There is a God."

This defining meeting realigned me in my spiritual quest. But it would take another seven years for me to surrender to the Son of that God.

COCAINE HELL

Back in Canada, Marie and I got married, and I started to work at the hospital as an orderly. But I also continued with the drug business and kept trying all kinds of spiritual paths—except Christianity. Marie would follow me in these discoveries, but on more than one occasion, she convinced me to get out before I went too far. You could have found us visiting a large hippy community in Tennessee or practicing kundalini yoga in an ashram in Ottawa or following a strict Japanese vegetarian yin and yang-balanced diet or studying the teachings of Indian gurus, Russian masters, or South American shamans. The list would be long and is not needed at this point.

Along with exploring spiritual paths, over time I progressed into the more destructive business of cocaine. That proved to be a downward spiral that brought great destruction in our lives. After two years of severe cocaine addiction, I was drowning in a sea of debt, was afraid to answer the phone, and kept a metal pipe by the door of my apartment to defend myself in case one of my creditors came calling. At that time, Marie was slipping toward depression, and we agreed it would be better to separate. I had nothing left to offer in a marriage. I basically spent every night on cocaine, not eating much, losing weight, and losing my sanity.

My younger brother, who had become a Christian and was living at the other end of the country, would call me from time to time to encourage me to give my life to Jesus. At some point in my wanderings, I had read the four Gospels, and I recognized that Jesus was indeed the Son of God, but I thought it was too late for me. During certain nights, I was visited by demons that would appear to me and mock me, saying I would never be saved, that Jesus couldn't do anything for me. And I believed it. I was twenty-seven years old and a complete failure.

SOBBING ON HIS SHOULDER

On the first Sunday of 1987, my brother suddenly opened the door and entered my apartment. He had just arrived from the West Coast. Without even greeting me, he said, "Put your coat on. I'm bringing you to church." On our way there, we stopped and picked up another one of our friends, Jocelyn, who, like me, was also into cocaine.

The church was a tiny place on a downtown street. My brother had found it in the phone book (that was before Google). There were maybe thirty people gathered, singing with their hands raised, following the lead of the suit-and-tie pastor with his accordion. It was a mix of country music and hymns. Not really my style. But I didn't care. There was warmth in the place. After fifteen to twenty minutes, I looked at Jocelyn, and I saw that his face was literally flooded with tears. *Wow, something's happening to him!* I thought to myself. Then suddenly my brother fell on the floor. People around us did not even flinch. The atmosphere was charged with *something*. Looking at the words of the songs on the screen, I saw the name *Jesus* constantly flashing before my eyes. And as you sometimes see in movies, the whole place started to vanish in a blur, with the sounds and music fading away.

It was then that I saw Him. He was standing in front of me, just a few steps away. I knew who He was. I could see the scars in His hands. He was so bright, and I felt like such a shameful sinner.

Lowering my head, I said, "Lord, why do you come to me now? Don't you know it's too late for me?"

He didn't say a word but took a step toward me.

"Jesus, didn't You hear what I just said? You are so holy and pure, and I'm so unclean. If You come closer to me, my filth will touch You and soil You. Don't come closer to me."

He never said a word and took one more step toward me.

In real panic, I implored, "Please, don't come closer. Can't You see my heart is dirty?"

Then He spoke, saying, "Give Me your heart."

In tears, I whispered, "Yes."

He took me into His arms, and I sobbed for a long time on His shoulder. All the sins of my life, the pains and the sorrows, gushed out of me as the waves of His love relentlessly passed through me.

I remember this like it was yesterday. Through my weeping I told Him, "I have never found a love like this anywhere, and if You are going to love me like this, I'll cling to You and never let You go. Wherever You go, I'll go with You. You'll never be able to get rid of me."

Then I found myself back in the church in the midst of worship.

THE APOSTOLIC BEGINS AND ENDS WITH JESUS

Why did I take time to share this testimony at the opening of a book on apostolic centers? I wanted to make a clear statement right from the start that the apostolic journey begins and ends with Jesus. He is the *Sent One* of the Father, the great *Apostolos* of our faith. He is and must remain the center.

This book is not about a new methodology for church growth, although in following the voice behind me, saying, "This is the way; walk in it" (see Isa. 30:21), I received step-by-step directions to transition our church into an apostolic center, which resulted in substantial growth, both in numbers and in spiritual capacity.

Sometimes the word *apostolic* brings to people's minds the picture of a well-oiled machine, with a plaque screwed on top with golden letters proclaiming, "Production and Efficiency." Once again, while we have a lot to gain by being better organized, my approach to this question tends to be more organic than industrial. I am more at ease with the new corporate trends that make room for meaningful relationships than with the classic business style. I just happen to think we can achieve more that way—with authentic communities divinely led.

In my attempts over the years to "build the church," on more than one occasion I lost sight of the simple call I had received in the beginning. We can easily be absorbed with working hard and using the gifts we were given to "get the job done." And there is always a possibility of being derailed, even when the train station is in sight. It was at such crucial moments in my pursuit of the apostolic ministry that the Lord would choose to draw near. In spite of the sounds produced by my noisy activity, His tender voice would reach me so clearly, "Do you remember what I asked you that day?"

"Yes, Lord, I do remember. How could I forget?"

"What was it? Tell Me," He would continue.

"You asked me...for my heart."

"Yes, that's right, and I have never changed My request. Your heart. Everything else has to be aligned with that."

This book, then, is about a heartbeat. And it all started in the setting of a tiny congregation worshipping the Lord.

MEETING THE CHURCH

I am a lover of the church. I have been since day one. I have never been able to separate Jesus from the church. I'm not sure He would like that anyway. And since what I'm writing here is to serve as a textbook for a new development in the church, I think it is important to give some background on my experience with the church. I understand that for some people just the mention of the word *church* is enough to bring back loads of painful memories. I am terribly sorry for that. But for me, church has been a wonderful refuge after despair and shame, a safe place of healing and restoration.

That day I met Jesus, I was instantly delivered from drug addiction, as if I had never touched drugs in my life. No cravings, no withdrawals, nothing. But there was still something very important that needed to happen.

After we left the building, as my feet touched the sidewalk, it was as if I came to my senses. *My wife!* I thought. *What have I done with my life?* I had dragged her with me down so many dead ends. How would she take this new Christian fad of mine? Even though we were separated, we were still keeping in contact with each other. Let's just say that Marie had enough compassion for me left in her to check on me from time to time. But to make a long story short, after hearing what I had to say, she went by herself to a Bible study on the Tuesday night, and there, as the pastor's wife was teaching from the Book of Romans, Marie's deep existential questions, that no one had ever answered, were explained. It became clear to her who we were, where we were coming from, where we were going, and why—if man was so intelligent—the world was in such a mess. After that we started attending every meeting, and it didn't take long before we got back together as a couple. The name of the church was *Eglise du Chemin du Calvaire* (Calvary Road Church), now changed to *Le Chemin* (The Way).

During the first few months we attended church, we basically wept through the services. We were overwhelmed by the sweet presence of God and by the love we saw all around. Week after week, upon returning home after church, I would ask Marie, "Did you see the light on the pastors' faces? They shine! And the love the people have? It's real. I tell you. They are for real." Many times it was like there was a thick cloud of anointing in the meeting, and I used to think, years later, after we sold that building, that the anointing must still be dripping from the walls.

Pastors Jean-Claude and Valerie had founded the church twelve years before we were saved. This was in the French province of Quebec, in Canada, in the midst of a strong Catholic culture, often hostile back then to what was considered a cult. We were located on Eddy Street, on one of the main blocks for bars and prostitution. There was often a lot of activity going on during the services, with people entering from the street at any given moment. But we had found our home.

Jean-Claude and Valerie became our true spiritual father and mother; they walked with us through healing and deliverance, growing pains, and everything. And we found new lifelong friends. In fact, we never left that church. That's right, the apostolic center we now lead is a development of that same church we came to more than twenty-five years ago. I have travelled extensively and visited hundreds of churches, but home is home. It is the same thing for Jean-Claude and Valerie; it's also still their home. How is this possible, someone may ask? Well, you will find out more about that as you keep reading.

AUTHENTIC COMMUNITY AND GLORY

There are two things I desired in life. The first was authentic community; the second was to see God's glory. Even before I was on this side of the cross, I had a longing in my heart for a different way of life. Back in the early '80s, it was not uncommon to talk about new types of communities. For me, it was more than talk. I had written a paper on a family-unit-based societal model that could have been implemented with just a bit of willingness to let go of some of our self-centeredness and our attachment to material possessions in order to embrace a more collective approach, trusting one another, far from the city, in houses we would build in the fields, etc. You see the picture. We smile today when we hear this. But the longing was real. There has to be an alternative to the ungodly society we inherited. There has to be a better way to live on this earth.

Where would the model come from? We don't have a great example from what we have tried through our various civilizations, except for maybe those few pages in the Book of Acts that appear as a lightning bolt in human history. What we see in the narrative of the first years of the church is the development of communities that were finally implementing heavenly codes of conduct. But it was only meant to be the beginning. And despite all the beauty we find today in the church, we still have to admit we have strayed so far from the original model that, in most cases, going back would still mean moving forward!

Authentic community living displays love, truth, forgiveness; it has the fragrance of the fruits of the Spirit. Glory manifests godly power and authority that is conducive to bringing transformation to society; it releases the strength of the gifts. But both components— authentic community living and glory—need to flow together if we ever want to see the divine pattern applied on the earth.

I struggled for many years, caught between my gratitude, love, and respect for the church and my indomitable thirst for more— stretched in the tension between what I saw in Acts and what we were experiencing in the present era. I desperately wanted to show people around us a model of society that would be attractive to the deepest longings of their hearts, just as the Lord becomes so attractive when correctly presented.

I have slowly come to the conclusion that a reformation of the church structure is inevitable if we want to convey the reality of heaven and advance the kingdom of God. Better preaching will not do it; more anointed altar calls will not do it; bigger rallies will not do it. The core structure of the church must be changed.

STRUCTURE FOLLOWS AND THEN SUSTAINS LIFE

What we're talking about here is life—receiving life, sustaining life, giving life. And there's no life without structure. As soon as life appears, a structure is created to sustain that life. This principle is described in 1 Corinthians 15:37–38:

> When you sow, you do not plant the body that will be, but just a seed, perhaps of wheat or of something else. But God gives it a body as he has determined, and to each kind of seed he gives its own body.

The seed contains the life, and when that precious seed is placed in the proper ground, the life it contains is manifested. But that life will be recognized by the form it will take. The *body* it comes wrapped with. The Lord gives to that life the body He ordained it to have according to His master plan. Each kind has its own body. But what comes first? The life or the body? The answer is the life. Then God gives it a body as He has determined. Neither exists without the other. But life comes first; then the structure follows to sustain life.

Another illustration for structure is what the Bible calls wineskins:

> And no one pours new wine into old wineskins. Otherwise, the wine will burst the skins, and both the wine and the wineskins will be ruined. No, they pour new wine into new wineskins (Mark 2:22).

The purpose of the wineskin is to host life. Without the wineskin, the wine cannot properly develop to reach its full potential. The whole process is for the wine, not the wineskin, but without the wineskin, there would be no wine. Structure follows life, then sustains it.

The problem is not with the wine but with the wineskin's capacity to expand. As wine is aging to become better and better, it doesn't remain static. This is the abundant life Jesus talks about in John 10:10. Life is ever growing, and the containers of life have to be able to adjust to the movement of the life they protect.

Every time we fight to preserve structure against life, we dry up. Every time we let life run without proper structure, we spill. Both ways are, unfortunately, too common. Some get drunk; some get dry. Let me present it this way: Structure is not the goal, but there's no lasting life without flexible wineskins.

DRYING UP IN THE MAINTENANCE MODE

Looking at the general picture of the church, I observed an emphasis on maintaining what we had received. Now, maintenance is not a bad thing in and of itself, but in terms of stewarding the investment Jesus entrusted to the church, maintenance alone won't meet the expectations. This is what the parable of the talents reveals with the master being displeased with the servant who did not bring an increase to what was given to him (see Matt. 25:24–27).

We need to realize the precious seed that was laid in the ground of the church is a living seed, destined to produce ever increasing harvests. Our harvesting system has to follow a strategic development plan. Fixing up and repainting the same old barn might be a fun activity to do with the kids on the weekends, but it will not adequately equip us to receive the incoming harvests. The new wine that's being poured into us is provoking an expansion in every area. Did I hear a crack?

Rigidity leads to death and vice versa. Why then are so many leaders caught in a rigid maintenance mode in the church? Why are so many fighting to preserve old structures rather than embracing life-yielding wineskins? I pondered these questions at various times as I was growing in the church environment. Here are a few potential answers I came to consider.

The Pastoral Paradigm

For the most part, the leadership of the church as we know it today has been given to either pastors or gifted administrators. By virtue of their calling, care and protection, rather than reformation, have become the *modus operandi*. This is easily understandable; not everyone is called to be a visionary or to feel excited at the prospect of breaking away from old models.

Here's how I see the global picture: The prophet perceives better pastures over the top of the next mountain. The apostle says, "Let's all go check it out!" The evangelist shares the word with everyone around. The pastor makes sure everybody has enough provisions for the road, while the teacher prepares maps and a description of the history of the land they will cross.

Let me make a clear point here: I am not in any way pointing the finger at the faithful pastors who are giving their lives to keep the legacy passed on to them for the future generations and always doing good around them while bringing souls to salvation and tending the flock. Their contribution to the kingdom of God is invaluable; they are heroes of the faith to be celebrated with high praises! All of us need a pastor in our lives; every church needs a pastor on the team. But when it comes to conquering new territory, the typical pastor is not so sure the idea of living under tents is very appealing. If it was up to him, most of the time he'd prefer for his flock to have the safety of staying home. That's in the DNA of his gift.

It would be totally unfair to lay on the pastors' shoulders, on top of all their demanding duties, the added responsibility of leading the church through a reformation process. The problem is not with the faithful pastors; they are fulfilling their mandate. What we need is for the apostolic reformation to get more traction in the reality of the church.

The Fear Factor

For other leaders, the thought of the unknown strikes the chord of fear. It is an unfortunate reality that many leaders are plagued with unresolved personal issues that produce tons of insecurities and paralyze them. Those leaders will try to control their environment as much as possible in order to avoid any change that could cause them to have to face their problems. For anyone who has been under the rule of an insecure leader, the experience has been stifling at best and abusive in the worst scenarios.

Hope Deferred

Then there is the great company of leaders who once saw the vision of a better church. They went wholeheartedly after that vision, passionately engaging in that sacred pursuit—only to eventually smash their faces full speed on the thick wall of the religious system. Many never recovered and eventually left organized Christianity. Others resigned themselves to a life of passionless ministry. Hope deferred. It makes the heart sick (see Prov. 13:12).

A Life Agent

When the structure doesn't serve the life, when it becomes so rigid it cannot sustain the movement of life within, the result is abortion or stillbirth. The structure destined to celebrate life becomes a casket—but only for a time. Life always finds a way to spring back, to burst out.

On the other hand, when the structure is the right one, with the appropriate qualities to contain without controlling, to sustain without directing, it allows life to follow its course. When it comes to the capacity to keep things moving and progressing, the church needs the leadership of the apostolic ministry—a life agent with authority to order structure after life.

CONFERENCES: THE GRAND ILLUSION

It can be reassuring, at first, to come to a church operating under a maintenance mode. There is stability and predictability, and if on top of that the pastors are loving, the combination is not bad at all. But it can also become boring after a while. Since as Bible readers we are exposed to story after story of supernatural adventures, it tends to awaken a spiritual hunger for more than the usual Sunday morning service provides. That hunger is placed inside us by the Lord to provoke us to change. It's a hunger to shake us out of complacency, to make us cry out, to drive us to action. It is meant to be a catalyst to produce a chain reaction that will reshape the church until abundant life becomes the norm. But when the rigid ecclesiastical structure is not willing to make room for change, that hunger looks for other ways to be satisfied.

What I'm going to write next may disturb some, but conferences have too often become a cop-out for unhealthy local church life, like a night at the movies to forget recession. A grand illusion.

Now don't get me wrong. I love conferences. I organize and host conferences. I speak at conferences. As I'm writing this, I just had a conference two weeks ago with Chuck Pierce, Peter Wagner, and Doug Schneider. It was brilliant. I'm a conference guy.

However, the problem comes when we use something good (a conference) as a substitute instead of fixing something that is broken (our church life). Then instead of changing our reality, we embrace the comforting illusion that we have another life, for a moment, until we go back home. I told you I was a lover of the church. This book is about church reformation. I have seen too many people running from conference to conference in the hope of getting a taste of what they don't find in their church.

I have also been part of noble and persevering efforts by church leaders to produce a reformation through the dynamics of conferences or gatherings of different kinds. While amazing prophetic acts were performed and corporate spiritual authority was exercised with results seen on a national scale, we were forced to admit in our debriefings that, in most cases, we were powerless to implement these dynamics in our home bases. So, we were experiencing a certain dimension in our conferences while continuing to live the same old life when we returned home. We did not know how to implement what we experienced in the conferences in our day-to-day lives, at least not in the type of churches we were used to.

I had the same feelings when we had special guests visiting the church. We would experience extraordinary meetings with them, where healings would happen or the prophetic would flow or some measure of glory would be manifested. But when they would leave, we would have to go back to our regular or normal services, and there was always a painful readjustment to go through. One time I told one of our guests, "We really appreciate your ministry, but after you're gone, we'll still be the same. Please teach us how you do it; tell us what goes through your mind when you minister, how you decide to move or not, how you hear God, and how you know what to do so we can learn to do it too after you're gone." I always wanted to see the glory not reserved for special occasions but as the inheritance of our daily lives. I always wanted our local churches to be able to host the glory.

In some circles, conferences have become like a parallel world. There is almost a new brand of ministers that we could call *conference apostles, conference prophets, conference preachers.* Without knowing it, we have produced a two-sided Christianity: *Wild Saturdays* and *Safe Sundays.* When I started to realize all that, I experienced a strong desire to see the apostolic ministers get their hands dirty in the soil of the local church in order to produce the kind of Sundays that would rock our cities.

HOLDING SERVICES OR IMPACTING THE CITY?

Who would like to go to a funeral every week? In some instances, this is what Sunday services have felt like. No wonder people have been looking to conferences for a breath of fresh air. But when I say that a new kind of Sunday needs to be produced, I'm talking of much more than a better church service. I'm talking about the apostolic capacity to position the body of Christ for a Jacob-style divine encounter. To gather a people at the very gate of heaven, to assemble together the very house of God (see Gen. 28:17).

This kind of gathering is a glory surge to empower and activate the people to literally invade their communities week after week with the gospel of the kingdom and the power to bring transformation. The strength of such Sundays needs to be linked to a systematic relational structure that is sustaining people in their action throughout the whole week. When this is in place, we witness a visitation from heaven every Sunday, and a glorious power is released to impact the city.

Why am I placing importance on Sundays? Is this not a religious approach? Religious or not, I've always liked to go to church on Sunday. In my first years at church, I sometimes had to work on Sundays as an orderly at the hospital. I would take my bicycle at lunch time, ride to the church, catch twenty minutes of the meeting, and then ride back to the hospital to finish my shift. When it comes to Sundays, I'll tell you what, instead of trying to reinvent the wheel, why not use what we have, do our homework, and see if a funeral procession can be changed into a resurrection march!

PARENTS DON'T LEAVE THEIR KIDS

But let me come back to where I left off in the story of my journey as a young believer. I had been in the church for twelve years. For nine of those years, I led our Christian school. It was a full-time position, even though the number of students was quite small. That period was my real hardcore training for ministry: theology readings, daily dealings with parents and kids, praying for finances. It broke me. It made me who I am today.

Pastor Jean-Claude had started to travel more and more outside the province, sharing about the French reality we lived in Quebec and the mission field we were in with the English part of the country. Over time, more doors continued to open, and with Valerie, his wife, their ministry as pastors of pastors gradually developed.

The church was still small, occupying the same storefront building. The work of the founding pastors had essentially been to lay a solid foundation and create a lasting core of believers. This being done successfully, the need for a transition started to be apparent. When a visiting prophet confirmed it was time to make a transition, Pastor Jean-Claude took a courageous step of faith and gathered the elders to discuss the situation. It was decided I would become the new pastor, while Jean-Claude and Valerie would pursue a full-time itinerant ministry. They were releasing the church entirely into my hands, no strings attached. But the most interesting thing is that the church remained their home base where they continued to be honored as Mom and Dad in the house. Marie and I became the leading pastors while they remained the founding pastors and our spiritual covering.

The transition went amazingly well for a number of reasons. First, I was their spiritual son and a true son of the house. Second, I made sure to always honor them publicly and privately. Third, we put in place measures to take care of them financially. Fourth, I respected the foundation they had established. Fifth, I included them on the leadership team. Sixth, they had enough spiritual and emotional maturity and security to release all control and let me lead; in fact, when I came up with changes I wanted to implement, their voices cheered me on, reassuring the elders, who at times struggled with my decisions.

It has been almost fifteen years since the passing of the baton, and our relationship is still going strong. When we made the apostolic shift a few years ago, Jean-Claude and Valerie were again my best supporters, and I included them in the newly formed apostolic team right beside Marie and me.

In following chapters, I am going to lay out the nuts and bolts of that second and more recent major transition we went through, the shift from a board of elders to an apostolic team and from a traditional local church to an apostolic center. But let me first finish the story of the beginnings.

THE CHURCH JESUS DREAMS OF

Becoming the lead pastor of the congregation I had grown with was quite exciting. It released me to start envisioning on another level. I am an idealist by nature. I tend to believe the best is always at hand. I started to look around and wonder, *What is the longing in God's heart? What is the church like that Jesus still dreams will come together?* How, as a community of believers, could we become a resting place for the presence of God and an active expression of His heart on the earth?

A Different Community

There is no doubt the Holy Spirit is building a community on the earth that's different from anything the world has ever seen. Even as the nation of Israel was to be, in many ways, a forerunner of that spiritual people to come, there was still a new company waiting to be formed when the fullness of time would be here.

The Lord wants to birth something on the earth through this company called the church. He wants to see the coming together of a new wineskin into which the new wine from heaven can be poured without being spilled. We are called to form this container where heaven can dwell on the earth.

I wasn't sure how this would all happen, but a few decisions we made along the way allowed us to progress toward what we would become.

Early Steps

I quickly made up my mind that we would not fight in any way to preserve a rigid structure. What that meant, I didn't totally know, but it sure sounded right! In Quebec, a mainly French-speaking province, the Catholic Church has been very strong since the beginning of the colony, and French protestant churches have been few, usually small, and mostly in survival mode. A lot of help had come from English Canada and America to start churches, teach, and support us. That help has been invaluable. The downside, though, is that the church setting presented to us did not always correspond to our DNA. In some ways, as a people and a culture exploring Christianity from a new angle, we were looking to find our identity, to define what the church should look like in our own setting.

With that in mind, I always insisted on welcoming liberty. I preferred erring on that side rather than on the side of rigidity and tight rules. That was not too foreign to the legacy of Pastor Jean-Claude, who had raised us with the sentence, "Here at the chapel"—we often referred to the church like that—"we don't have any program; we follow the Holy Spirit." I wanted to continue to develop a culture of freedom, and that sometimes looked a bit chaotic. Let's say it was "managed disorder," certainly more Latin-style than proper Anglo-Saxon order. Rules have a customized definition for me; they are the best option, most of the time. Because of that mindset, I wanted us to have the fragrance of love, a community led by the heart, not by a church manual.

I also shared with the congregation that we needed to focus on training and releasing people, on raising disciples (not just converts), and on developing leaders. That change would eventually release an explosion, but when we started on that track, it was an ideal. I had no idea how we could accomplish that. We were a church of about fifty people, with people who had been in the church together for a long time. I mention this to encourage all those readers who can identify with a similar situation. Lift up your eyes and look; your destiny is rising on the horizon.

Then after a while, I realized we needed to break through with high praises. The spiritual atmosphere of the province was so oppressive that we needed aggressive worship to pierce the thick depressive blanket in the air. Some songs or worship styles we heard on tapes (remember those—before CDs and iTunes!) were okay for other areas of the world, where revival had cleared the air, but they could not help us here. We had to develop warrior worship until we broke through the darkness.

Finally, I took a stand that we would become the most generous church around. Like many others, we were used to being on the receiving end of things, but I wanted to plant our tent pegs on the giving end and refuse the poverty mindset. We applied this in many ways. We started to give big offerings to guest speakers (even beyond our capacity; I would tell our bookkeeper to withhold my own salary if needed), and we became strong contributors to any church events in the area, even though we were still a small church.

Generosity is not mainly a matter of money; it's a heart attitude. We developed a giving and serving mindset toward other churches and toward the city. I'll always remember one of the festivals we organized in a park, serving the population with free lunches, a bicycle repair shop, and an honorary tribute to special citizens and dignitaries of the city. One afternoon, we had invited a church from the neighborhood to join us in the worship and outreach. When the time came to speak, I asked the pastor in private to address the people and invite them to his church. He couldn't believe I would do that, since we had organized and paid for everything and never asked for a penny from his church. Also, he was from a more conservative kind of church, and maybe he wasn't sure he should step on our kind of platform. So, I did the speaking, and I promoted his church, telling the people if they were looking for a place to worship, his church was a good one, and I recommended it!

PART OF THE NAR WITHOUT EVEN KNOWING

In the mid '90s, C. Peter Wagner came up with the term New Apostolic Reformation (NAR), based on his careful observation of the movement of the Holy Spirit in the church, movement that showed great progress with specific conditions. After a few attempts at finding a name that could describe what he was seeing, he eventually came up with NAR, a name people started to use and that finally stuck. I know some people still think it is a movement he created or an organization he established. When you realize the magnitude of what NAR describes and its grassroots dynamics, it is rather funny some people would think that way, but I'll chalk it up to being misinformed. So many things have been said about it, but here I'm going to give you one more scoop: You may be part of the NAR and not even know it!

Our congregation had been established by a godly couple who definitely had an apostolic mantle on their lives. The structure of the church might have been traditional, but in those years, not many other models existed. What was truly remarkable, though, was their vision for a family and for the presence of the Lord (authentic community and glory).

I represented the next generation, privileged to stand on the solid foundation faithfully laid before us, with the support of a spiritual father and mother, at a time when great revelation was released in the body of Christ, as the new apostolic age and the kingdom mindset intersected. We couldn't have put the right terminology on it back then; we were just excited to love Jesus and apply our hearts and minds to finding ways for His kingdom to come in our lives. Without knowing it, we were entering a reformation. Like countless others, we were launched into the New Apostolic Reformation before we had ever heard about it. This led us to the journey this book is about.

Before I go into the details of how we transitioned into an apostolic center, I will present a better understanding of some of the main apostolic dynamics.

CHAPTER 2
The Apostolic Mandate

WHO SENT YOU?

So now, go. I am sending you to Pharaoh to bring my people the Israelites out of Egypt." But Moses said to God, "Who am I, that I should go to Pharaoh and bring the Israelites out of Egypt?" And God said, "I will be with you…" Moses said to God, "Suppose I go to the Israelites and say to them, 'The God of your fathers has sent me to you,' and they ask me, 'What is his name?' Then what shall I tell them?" God said to Moses, "I AM WHO I AM. This is what you are to say to the Israelites: 'I AM has sent me to you' (Exod. 3:10–14).

Moses is the most prominent apostle of the Old Testament. Two forty-year seasons were needed to prepare him for his calling, but finally, in front of a burning bush, the commissioning took place. In that commissioning we can clearly see the three key elements of any apostolic venture: a sender, a sent one, and a mission. That's what the dialogue between God and Moses was all about.

The mission was no surprise: getting the people out of Egypt. Moses had not been able to get this out of his mind for the last forty years. Nowhere do we see him question the validity of the mission, but he was not so sure he was the right one to carry it out. His failure in Egypt forty years earlier was still fresh in his mind, but this time God told him, "I will be with you."

Moses had learned a few lessons over the years. He knew what had weight and what didn't. He knew that when he went to the people to explain his mission, they would have but one question, "Who sent you?" That's the apostolic question. And Moses was, by then, well aware of the importance of that question. Isn't it interesting that an eighty-year-old man would be asked by mostly younger men, "Who sent you?" Isn't that the type of question we would be more likely to ask a teenager or a young man coming on an errand? But Moses knew it was the key that unlocks the power for any mission. And God knew it too. So He said to Moses, and I paraphrase, "Go ahead, Moses. Go ahead and tell them *who* is sending you!

JESUS OUR APOSTLE

But when the set time had fully come, God sent his Son... (Gal. 4:4).

Timing is everything. My brother-in-law, Gigi, used to tell me, "The right thing at the wrong time is still the wrong thing." He would also say, before bursting with laughter, "There's a big difference between now and *right now.*"

Moses fulfilled the mandate for his hour. Hebrews 3:5 tells us, "Moses was faithful as a servant in all God's house, bearing witness to what would be spoken by God in the future." This *future* is the fullness of time Galatians 4:4 talks about. When the time had fully come, apostolic birth pangs were finally released, and God sent His Son!

Moses was faithful as a servant in the house, "But Christ is faithful as the Son over God's house" (Heb. 3:6). This is why Jesus is the apostle and high priest whom we confess (see Heb. 3:1), and is "found worthy of greater honor than Moses" (Heb. 3:3). Throughout all our discussions and efforts to build apostolically, we need to keep our eyes on Jesus, knowing "the builder of a house has greater honor than the house itself" (Heb. 3:3).

In his first letter, the apostle John shared, "And we have seen and testify that the Father has sent his Son to be the Savior of the world" (1 John 4:14). Again, we have a sender, a sent one, and a mission. Let's explore the meaning of this before going farther.

INVADE, OCCUPY, AND TRANSFORM

Pax Romana

The main Greek words used in the New Testament about the concept of the apostolic are *apostolos* (the noun), *apostello* (the verb), and *apostole* (a noun both for apostleship and apostle). The definition of *apostole,* as found in *Strong's Concordance,* contains some very interesting insights:

1. of the sending off of a fleet
2. of consuls with an army, i.e. of an expedition

The authors of the New Testament were living under the Roman Empire, and their choice of words reflected their understanding of that reality. When Paul said Jesus was the *apostle* we confess, he could see beyond the religious context and was drawing from the culture of his day. What he saw was the picture of a whole fleet leaving Rome to conquer foreign coastal lands or a consul advancing with his army, the Roman banner floating high, ready to take new territories for the emperor.

The term for apostle is a military one; the setting is that of a conquest, both under the Greek and Roman Empires. We'll use the Roman example for our study.

Rome was led by emperors who constantly went to war until all the known world was conquered, which happened under Octavius, who then inaugurated a two-hundred-year period of peace called the *Pax Romana*. The reason for that period of peace lies not only in the fact that all countries had been conquered, but because the Romans were able to establish a Roman way of life in those conquered countries, with their armies staying permanently in a country after an invasion to occupy the place. The Roman Empire included what we today call Western Europe, the Middle East, and North Africa. Many of those societies benefited from the Roman rule imposed on them, for example by being introduced to Roman public baths, roads, water supplies, housing, and a stability that made life better for the populations.

There were thus three strategic phases to a successful Roman conquest: invade, occupy, and transform. The emperor sent a fleet or an army, led by a consul, with a clear mission. This "apostle" had all the power of the emperor delegated to him to lead the operations and proceed with the invasion. Once the victory was secured, he would install his leaders and troops all over the country to occupy it and govern it, not only to keep the population from rebelling but to introduce them to new laws, new infrastructures, a new culture, and a new type of society. So, when the emperor would come to visit his conquered territories, he would find they had become a real extension of Rome and feel right at home. The same apostolic dynamics are at the core of God's redemptive plan for the earth.

A Beachhead

Jesus left heaven, sent from His Father, with the mission and authority to invade the world, occupy it, and transform it. In other words, Jesus was sent to bring the rule of the kingdom of God on earth as it is in heaven—to prepare a dwelling place for the holy presence, a home for God with men.

The victory of Jesus on the cross and His resurrection established an impregnable and permanent beachhead from where His apostolic armies are constantly being sent forth to invade the earth with the gospel of the kingdom.

Fill the Earth

As populations are receiving salvation, it is very important for the church to understand the need to properly occupy the newly added territories. What the Lord told Moses on that topic deserves to be acknowledged. Talking about the nations Israel would need to conquer in the Promised Land, the Lord said:

> But I will not drive them out in a single year, because the land would become desolate and the wild animals too numerous for you. Little by little I will drive them out before you, until you have increased enough to take possession of the land (Exod. 23:29–30).

This passage makes it clear that there is no use in extending our borders if we're not ready to occupy what we conquer. In fact, when we fail to occupy the territories we have conquered, it is dangerous because we leave the door open for another type of enemy, worse than the first, to come in and quickly multiply. Jesus made a similar analogy in Matthew 12:43–45 when He described the house that had been cleansed but not occupied:

> When an impure spirit comes out of a person, it goes through arid places seeking rest and does not find it. Then it says, 'I will return to the house I left.' When it arrives, it finds the house unoccupied, swept clean and put in order. Then it goes and takes with it seven other spirits more wicked than itself, and they go in and live there. And the final condition of that person is worse than the first. That is how it will be with this wicked generation.

God knows nothing remains empty for long. An empty place is an invitation to be filled. The question is, what or who will fill the void? The Lord is a filling God. He filled the tabernacle and then the temple with His glory, and ultimately He will fill the whole earth with the knowledge of His glory (see Hab. 2:14). Christ wants us (as members of His body) first to "be filled to the measure of all the fullness of God" (Eph. 3:19) and the church to truly become "the fullness of him who fills everything in every way" (Eph. 1:23), so that we will be able to pick up and fulfill the original mandate given to Adam and Eve to "fill the earth and subdue it" (Gen. 1:28).

The Ultimate Transformation

The plan for creation was to establish a habitation on earth where God would share His authority with people created in His image. The plan for salvation is to bring us back to the original mandate in order for us to finally fulfill it. Jesus didn't come to open a way for us to escape from earth but to empower us to take over and see His dominion among people established through us (we'll discuss that in chapters 8 and 9). This calls for a radical transformation of all aspects of society. Everything that pertains to the lives of people together (our societies and cultures) and our relationship with nature needs to be brought into alignment with the divine plan. This is the task that is still ahead of us as a church until we see that "the kingdom of the world has become the kingdom of our Lord and of his Messiah" (Rev. 11:15). This is the apostolic mandate.

APOSTOLIC SENDING

The One Who Sent

John, the disciple whom Jesus loved, seemed to understand more than anyone the apostolic nature of the relationship the Father shared with His Son. His writings are filled with the deepest and most sacred revelations on this union.

The way we refer to someone, the name we use to do it or the attributes we attach to that name, most often gives meaningful insight both on how we define the nature of the one we are talking about and how we position ourselves in relation to that same person.

In the gospel of John alone, when Jesus talked about His Father,

He used expressions like "the Father who sent Me," and "the one who sent Him" more than twenty times. For example, in John 5:37, "The Father who sent me has himself testified concerning me." We understand that for Jesus, the Father is not only the Father, but *the Father who sent Him*. Here the verb for *sent* is *pempo*, a synonym of *apostello* that we see in the verse just prior to it, "For the works that the Father has given me to finish—the very works that I am doing—testify that the Father has sent [*apostello*] me" (John 5:36).

Another example is found in John 16:5, where Jesus talked about His departure, "Now I am going to *him who sent me*. None of you asks me, 'Where are you going?'" (emphasis added). Here again, when Jesus wanted to speak about His Father, He chose to link Him to the apostolic dimension and referred to Him as *Him who sent Me*.

The One He Sent

Having seen that Jesus called His Father *the one who sent*, it's not surprising to find that He also referred to Himself in the same way—as *the one He sent*. When we add verse 38 to John 5:37, we see Jesus put the two together:

> And the Father *who sent me* has himself testified concerning me. You have never heard his voice nor seen his form, nor does his word dwell in you, for you do not believe *the one he sent* [*apostello*] (emphasis added).

This is also found in John 6:29, "Jesus answered, 'The work of God is this: to believe in the one he has sent [*apostello*].'"

FATHER AND SON LINKED IN APOSTOLIC UNITY

A lot could be said about the unity of the Father and the Son. The relationship they share is a major key to the whole redemptive plan that is still unfolding. That unity is so deep that when Jesus got closer to the cross, John said, "The hour had come for him to leave this world and go to the Father" (John 13:1). Jesus was leaving a *place* to go to a *person*, leaving the created world to go back to the Creator.

In John 7:33–34, Jesus explained it this way:

I am with you for only a short time, and then *I am going to the one who sent me*. You will look for me, but you will not find me; and *where I am*, you cannot come (emphasis added).

In other words, He was saying where He *is* (present tense) is not a place but a person, and that person is the *one who sent Him*. He said, "Now I am going to him who sent me" (John 16:5). It all makes sense when we consider that Jesus came, not from a place but from the Father:

I came from the Father and entered the world; now I am leaving the world and going back to the Father (John 16:28).

Jesus came *from* the Father and then went *back to* the Father. What was in between? His apostolic mission: entering and leaving the world. The Father and Son are eternally linked in apostolic unity. An apostolic season has been inserted in the timeless dwelling of the Father and the Son and grafted to them. Just as the Son of God became flesh, eternity accepted time. The sending factor is a dynamic movement that links heaven and earth in divine destiny.

The apostolic dimension, the sending factor, has then become an integral part of the unity of the Son and the Father. This is why Jesus says that if we believe in Him, we don't believe only in Him but also in the one who *sent* Him (see John 12:44), and if we look at Him we in fact see the one who *sent* Him (see John 12:45).

The verse that really brings all this to a point is John 17:21:

That all of them may be one, Father, just as you are in me

and I am in you. May they also be in us so that the world may *believe that you have sent me* (emphasis added).

As recorded in John 17, in His last few moments before He was arrested, Jesus prayed five times for our unity. His prayer was that our unity would be modeled after the unity He had with His Father. But what is extraordinary to me is the purpose of that unity: that the world may believe the Father had sent Him!

At other times, Jesus mentioned that we needed to believe in the one whom God had sent (see John 6:29), in the Son of Man (see John 9:35), or simply in Him. But in John 17:21 (and also in verse 23), at the moment of the deepest revelation of the unity He had with His Father, He prayed it would cause the world to believe the Father had sent Him.

It's as if Jesus is saying that if we want to know Him in the depth of His union with the Father, we need to have a revelation of the mission that linked both of them before the foundation of the world (see Rev. 13:8). We cannot separate Jesus from the apostolic commission He received from the Father.

DYNAMICS OF OUR OWN SENDING

Once we understand the unity between the Father and the Son, we realize the Great Commission (see Matt. 28:16–20) is not only a sending off to action but also an invitation to relationship and partnership. Just as Jesus had been sent, we too are also sent in the same fashion:

As you *sent* [*apostello*] *me* into the world, I have *sent* [*apostello*] *them* into the world (John 17:18, emphasis added).

In other words, if I could paraphrase, Jesus was saying to the Father, "As You have *made Me an apostle*, I have *made them apostles* to the world." And in the same way that the sending factor or the apostolic dynamic links the Father and the Son together, it also links us to Jesus and, through Jesus, to the Father:

> Very truly I tell you, whoever accepts anyone I send accepts
> me; and whoever accepts me accepts the one who sent me
> (John 13:20).

The implications of this are extraordinary. When asked by Philip
to show the Father, Jesus answered,

> Anyone who has seen me has seen the Father. How can you
> say, "Show us the Father"? Don't you believe that I am in
> the Father, and that the Father is in me? (John 14:9–10)

Then a bit farther on in the conversation, Jesus told His disciples
the time would come when we would realize that not only is He
in His Father, but we are also in Him (Jesus), and He (Jesus) is in
us (see John 14:20). Even more, as the Son is in us, the Father is
also present, and they will come and make their home with us (see
John 14:23).

If the result of Jesus and the Father being together was that
anyone who saw Jesus saw the Father, then the result of us being
with Jesus needs to be that anyone who sees us is seeing Jesus. The
apostolic church of the twenty-first century is starting to experience
the presence of God with such depth that we will be able to answer
those still doubting by saying, "How can you say, 'Show us Jesus'?
Anyone who has seen the church has seen Jesus."

APOSTOLIC PROVISION: FUSION WITH THE ONE WHO SENT

Eating is a great thing. I remember the days when our two sons
were just little boys. Once I took them fishing, and before we left,
Marie made us a little bag lunch that my youngest carried like a
treasure in the boat. We had just left the dock, with the cottage still
in view behind us, when I heard an eager voice asking, "Is it time
to eat our lunch now, Dad?"

Provision comes with the commission. The truth of the matter is that no one can work indefinitely without eating. Our reserves are eventually depleted, our strength dwindles, our stomachs start to ache, and we show our grumpy side. We came into this world already able to produce energy. All we need to make it work is a regular intake of appropriate food.

When pressed by His disciples to eat, Jesus said to them, "I have food to eat that you know nothing about" (John 4:32). "My food," said Jesus, "is *to do the will of him who sent me* and to finish his work" (John 4:34, emphasis added). This gives us an interesting perspective on apostolic provision. John 6:57 takes it even farther:

Just as the living Father sent me and I live because of the Father, so the one who feeds on me will live because of me.

Allow me to propose my own amplified version like this:

Just as the living [*zao*] Father sent me [apostolic sending— *apostello*] and I live [*zao*] *because of* [by—apostolic provision] the Father, so the one who feeds on me [eats my flesh and drinks my blood] will live [*zao*] *because of* [by—apostolic provision] me.

The flesh and the blood of Jesus are true spiritual sustenance, and as we partake in this apostolic provision, as we dwell and keep dwelling in Him, we experience a fusion of life with the one who sent us. The life of the Father, which is poured in the Son whom He sent and feeds Him, produces the life of the Son that is poured in us, the ones whom He sent, and feeds us.

APOSTOLIC SOURCE OF AUTHORITY

There's really only one question that needs to be answered on the earth, "Who has authority here?" All other questions find their resolution in this one. This is the question our enemies immediately assess in any new confrontation. This is the question everyone is concerned with whenever a crisis occurs. So, who's in charge?

In a created world, the ultimate source of authority has, by necessity, to come from outside, from the creator who brought that creation to existence. I say the ultimate source or the original source because any authority not proceeding from that source is doomed to dry up and be replaced—or contested and displaced. This is the problem the devil is encountering and the reason why the span of time he has in the world is limited.

Jesus, on the other hand, shared apostolic unity with the original source, and this is why His kingdom will see no end (see Rev. 11:15). He made it clear that He was from above, that He was not from this world (see John 8:23). His source was from a higher realm, and He operated in strict alignment with it, "But he who sent me is trustworthy, and what I have heard from him I tell the world" (John 8:26).

The apostolic pattern can be summarized by this: a word sent from heaven causing the earth to align with it. Whoever carries this word carries authority. It's a word that shakes and shapes. It declares, "On earth as it is in heaven" (Matt. 6:10). Jesus was the incarnation of the word, and before He left, He gave His apostles the words (*rhema*) of eternal life (see John 6:68) He had received from His Father, ensuring they would continue His apostolic mission with the same authority He Himself carried:

> Now they know that everything you have given me comes from you. For *I gave them the words* [*rhema*] *you gave me* and they accepted them. They knew with certainty that I came from you, and they believed that you sent me (John 17:7–8, emphasis added).

It's under this transfer of the word that we have authority to, "Go into all the world and preach the good news to all creation" (Mark 16:15). Paul understood this question very well when he wrote, "And how can they preach unless they are sent [*apostello*]? As it is written, 'How beautiful are the feet of those who bring good news!'" (Rom. 10:15). Those who are sent to invade, occupy, and transform are united with the Father, sustained by His provision, and advance with His delegated authority.

Now, let's look at the basic strategy both Jesus and Paul established to fulfill their apostolic mandates.

AN APOSTLE SURROUNDED BY A TEAM

Jesus

Whenever someone wants to launch an invasion on a given territory or nation, the first thing he does is gather the team or troops he needs for the operation. Depending on the task ahead, this team will vary in composition and size, but there is no hope of success without a team.

Forming a team was even a priority for Jesus, even though He came from heaven and was sent by the Father, was filled with the Holy Spirit, and had authority and a clear vision. It was so important that, before choosing twelve men for His core team from the group of disciples who had started to follow Him, Jesus spent the whole night in prayer (see Luke 6:12–13).

In choosing the disciples, He wanted to establish both a relational base that would be a prototype for future apostolic ministries and a functional unit capable of carrying out the mandate to establish the kingdom of God on earth. I take this from Mark 3:14–15:

> He appointed twelve that they might be with him [relational base] and that he might send them out to preach and to have authority to drive out demons [functional capacity].

We see in Luke 8:1 that those twelve apostles traveled with Jesus from town to town as He proclaimed the good news of the kingdom of God. But the next two verses show us that there were also quite a few women with the team, supporting Jesus out of their own means. This and other passages allow us to see that while the twelve were without any doubt the main players around Jesus, the team was in fact, at various times, larger than that, welcoming people who were not necessarily apostles but who nonetheless contributed significantly to the ministry. For this reason, I believe it is more accurate to talk about an apostolic team surrounding Jesus rather than a team of apostles. This is the terminology I adopted for this book, as it also fits very well for the teams that Paul developed.

Paul

Paul was certainly one of the apostles who qualified for what Ephesians 2:20 speaks about. He was instrumental in building the foundation of the church on the right cornerstone. If I could say it like this, Jesus laid out the initial model, the church of Jerusalem represented the intermediate stage, and Paul took it to the next level. But when he started, I'm sure Paul didn't have a clue of what it would become.

Barnabas was the one who first saw the tremendous potential in Paul. He went to Tarsus to look for him and brought him to Antioch, where together they taught in the church for a whole year.

At that church, Paul and Barnabas were set apart, according to the request of the Holy Spirit (see Acts 13:1–3) and sent to inaugurate a new apostolic era that we read about in the rest of the Book of Acts. Paul only knew the Holy Spirit was sending him to preach with Barnabas, but they ended up establishing communities of believers and appointing people as elders. They then returned to report to Antioch, their sending base. After being there for a while, Paul took another trip to see how everybody was doing, this time with Silas, a prophet.

To make a long story short, as this developed from city to city and from trip to trip, apostolic teams, with Paul, established new communities of believers everywhere. Those teams moved with the great flexibility that is so characteristic of new wineskins. They linked the newly formed churches into networks, and in locations that were more strategic, Paul stayed there long enough to establish apostolic centers. This original pattern is the one we see the Holy Spirit reactivating today.

APOSTLES, TEAMS, CENTERS, NETWORKS

When the New Apostolic Reformation started to be acknowledged in the mid '90s, the attention was mainly on the restoration of the ministry and the person of the apostle. What people didn't realize at first was that apostles don't come alone. They usually surround themselves with apostolic teams, establish apostolic centers, and lead apostolic networks. That, in a nutshell, is what we discovered at Le Chemin during the two-year journey that brought us through a complete transition from a traditional local church to an apostolic center.

In the next chapter, we'll look in more detail at the apostolic pattern we see in Acts, and in Chapter 4 I will walk you step-by-step through our transition process. You'll gain more understanding of the significance of the emergence of apostolic centers today, and for those of you gifted with an apostolic calling, it will provide you with some guidance to move ahead.

CHAPTER 3

Discovering Apostolic Centers

THE CHURCH IN JERUSALEM

A Model in Heaven

The two years of our apostolic transition were 2010 and 2011. I am one of those church leaders who seeks the Lord before every new year for a theme. For 2010, the theme I received was *The Kingdom of Heaven Is Near* (see Matt. 10:7). There was a great hunger in my heart to see the church live a life that aligned more closely with what Jesus preached and demonstrated, "Heal the sick, raise the dead, cleanse those who have leprosy, drive out demons. Freely you have received, freely give" (Matt.10:8). This caused me to think that if Jesus was saying the kingdom of heaven was near, there had to be a model in heaven He wanted to see reproduced here on earth, and our mandate was to continue this very work He had started. Just as Moses was instructed to build the tabernacle according to the model he was shown on the mountain, there had to be a model Jesus desired His church to incarnate.

A Model on the Earth

As the year progressed, I was led to examine the original model we have for the church, as it is recorded in the Book of Acts. As a church, we spent considerable time looking over and over the first chapters, with an emphasis on the description of the early church life found in Acts 2:41–47. In that passage, verse 42 became foundational to us with its four pillars for the church:

> They devoted themselves to the apostles' teaching and to the fellowship, to the breaking of bread and to prayer.

What I really wanted was to discover the type of community the church should endeavor to become. My reasoning was that if we could return to the original model, we would meet the conditions for the presence of God to dwell more fully among us, and this would in turn release us to experience the kind of church life we read about in Acts. So, week after week we studied the model of the early church of Jerusalem, inspired by what the very end of chapter 2 reports: "And the Lord added to their number daily those who were being saved" (Acts 2:47).

Toward the end of the year, I pushed the reading farther and discovered the church of Antioch. I had already read the whole Book of Acts many times just in that year—not mentioning the years before—but this time, when I came to chapter 13, for the first time I saw the huge significance of the shift it reported and how, from the initial sending of Paul and Barnabas, the rest of the Book of Acts burst with apostolic expansion. We were certainly not finished with that book!

FROM JERUSALEM TO ANTIOCH

The theme for 2011 was *Back to Acts*. Having spent a good portion of 2010 in Acts 2:41–47, we had developed a clear picture of the internal dynamics of a spirit-filled community. We had been practicing authentic fellowship for many years, feeding on the apostles' teaching (the Word of God), having passionate worship and prayer, all the while keeping the death and resurrection of Jesus central, but somehow the study of the early church in Jerusalem crystallized for us what a healthy home base should be—a believers' nuclear church, a spiritual house where we love one another as we love the Lord. Now that this strong foundation had been confirmed, the Lord opened our eyes to the next phase of development that unfolded in the church of Antioch. From that discovery, we progressed step-by-step all year toward an understanding of what apostolic teams and apostolic centers were. In fact, right from my first message of the year to the congregation, I announced that in 2011 we wanted to become like Antioch: an apostolic base.

The Acts 13 Shift

What I was seeing in chapter 13 was the Holy Spirit intervening in a sovereign way to shift the course of the church forever:

> While they were worshiping the Lord and fasting, the Holy Spirit said, "Set apart for me Barnabas and Saul for the work to which I have called them" (Acts 13:2).

That was a defining moment in the history of the early church. From that point on, the face of the church would change, and a new development strategy would be born with a new methodology. I became fascinated by the narrative of Paul's apostolic journeys and the exuberant life that was released among the early believers in the ever increasing number of cities where the gospel was preached and congregations were established.

The special role and position of the church of Antioch stood out with such clarity! There was a new dynamic at work that I hadn't seen in the church of Jerusalem. From Antioch, Paul and Barnabas were *sent* by the Holy Spirit; Antioch was a sending base. The way the Holy Spirit sent them was through the leaders of the church, who laid hands on the two apostles (see Acts 13:3); this established the model of how we should set people apart and send them out to minister. After Paul and Barnabas had completed their work, they returned to Antioch, and "they gathered the church together and reported all that God had done through them and how he had opened the door of faith to the Gentiles" (Acts 14:27). Antioch was definitely a new type of church, since it was sending teams on apostolic missions. For Paul, it would remain his first apostolic base and a model he would get inspiration from to develop strong apostolic centers in other parts of the world.

GOING BACK TO JUMP FARTHER

I have heard a number of people say that Acts is not a model to imitate, that we are not called to go back, but to go forward, and that what we see in Acts was the starting point, not the goal we should aim toward. I personally find those declarations too general and idealistic to be of much practical use. They may sound right when we first hear them, but unless we contextualize what they mean, they will not help us to move forward.

A Grand Restoration Project

God has been working on a grand restoration project for a while. First there is the "restoration of all things" that Peter talked about in Acts 3:21. That would include the reinstatement of mankind as the head of creation and the renewing of the earth. For that part, the second Adam had to go back to where the first Adam had dropped the ball, deal with the original sin, crush the head of the serpent, taste death, and then enter back into life. He now lives forever and ever, and we live with Him. But He first had to go back.

Then there is the restoration of David's fallen tent (see Acts 15:16–17), and then the restoration of the kingdom of Israel (see Acts 1:7–8); these are all movements to go back in time, pick up what has been broken, fix it, and then once again move forward to fulfill God's original intent.

When we observe the second half of the history of the church, we also see a progressive restoration of different truths and practices taking place over long periods of time. This restoration has accelerated in our day. To name just a few: there was the restoration of the Word of God in the hands of the people in the fourteenth century; the restoration of the truth of salvation by faith in the sixteenth century; the restoration of the baptism of the Holy Spirit at the turn of the twentieth century; and within the last hundred years or so, the restoration of—among other things—the ministry of healing, the office of the prophet, and the office of the apostle. Like I said, these are just a few examples. I am not trying to establish a list here. My point is that God is restoring what was lost with the goal of moving us ahead.

Restoring Apostolic Christianity

When we want to take part in the restoration of apostolic Christianity, a good place to start is by studying the Book of Acts. If we were in a more advanced stage today than what we see in Acts, it would be understandable that we wouldn't be interested in going back in time; however, the fact is the church is in real need of an apostolic reformation because we departed from the original model a long time ago. Since that is the case, going back means moving ahead!

We have probably all watched the Olympics and seen an athlete take a small step back before he starts running at full speed to finally take his leap for a long jump or triple jump. That's what *Back to Acts* was for us at Le Chemin; we took a small step back to jump farther. If we want to move beyond what we see in Acts and fulfill the apostolic mandate for the church, we need to first align ourselves with the original model. There is an initial step back and then a moving forward.

So, for a whole year, we lived with Paul and traced back our roots along the way. What we discovered accelerated the paradigm shift that had started for us the year before. The difference we saw between the *pastoral church model* and the *apostolic center model* produced a radical shift in our view of the church, which in turn brought us to change our governing structures and adopt new leadership practices.

Let's examine further the original picture we see developing around Paul's journeys.

EARLY APOSTOLIC EXPANSION

What are the key elements we can extract from the narrative of the apostolic journeys that started with the opening of Acts 13 and went on from there?

An Initial Apostolic Base

First, there was an initial apostolic base in Antioch. I call it an apostolic base because its leadership contained the foundational gifts of apostles (Paul and Barnabas) and prophets, and the pastoral gift of teachers (Acts 13:1; for more information on the foundational gifts, see Eph. 2:20 and 1 Cor. 12:28). I say *initial* base because it was the first sending base of its kind (a prototype). The Holy Spirit chose Antioch to launch a new phase of the apostolic, and for many years Antioch remained Paul's home base, to which he kept returning.

The Holy Spirit Is in Charge

Second, we see that the Holy Spirit was in charge. He was the one choosing men and sending them (see Acts 13:2–4). The whole venture was His initiative. He kept leading it all the way.

A Chosen Man

Third, there was Paul, a man who stood out among all the others. He's the key apostolic figure in that story. He went from city to city, from region to region, preaching the good news and making disciples (see Acts 14:21) among both Jews and Gentiles. He saw healings and miracles, faced resistance and persecution, and portrayed a joyful perseverance that still inspires us two thousand years later.

Apostolic Teams

Fourth, Paul very rarely worked by himself; most of the time we see him with companions. For his first trip, he left with Barnabas and John (see Acts 13:5); for his second trip, he started with Silas (see

Acts 15:40) and soon added Timothy (see Acts 16:1–3). Sometime after that, Luke joined the team. How do we know that? It's because starting with verse 10, the author of the book suddenly included himself in the story by using *we*. Who was that writer? Luke. By his third trip, we see quite an increase in the size of the apostolic team that Paul led. Take Acts 20:4–6 for example:

> He was accompanied by Sopater son of Pyrrhus from Berea, Aristarchus and Secundus from Thessalonica, Gaius from Derbe, Timothy also, and Tychicus and Trophimus from the province of Asia. These men went on ahead and waited for us at Troas. But we sailed from Philippi after the Feast of Unleavened Bread, and five days later joined the others at Troas, where we stayed seven days.

Not only were there more and more people, but we also see them being dispatched to different places, with different itineraries and schedules, before they eventually reunited later along the way. We could add people like Priscilla and Aquila to the list as well, as they travelled with Paul only occasionally but could nonetheless be counted as part of his team (see Acts 18:1–19). In fact, as the work developed, it would be more accurate to speak of apostolic teams, plural, rather than just one team.

The composition of the apostolic teams included a variety of gifts. Paul was the main leader, but there were also other apostles like Timothy and Titus (at one point both of them were given the responsibility to set a church in order, a clear apostolic mandate); prophets like Silas; a writer (Doctor Luke); and many others whose roles are not clearly defined for us. But we see enough variation to conclude that an apostolic team is a multi-gifted company of people surrounding a God-sent apostle on an apostolic mission.

Communities of Believers

Fifth, as Paul and his companions moved from city to city, they organized the new believers into communities. People were not only saved *from* something but also *into* something. They were added to a spiritual family.

When the time came for Paul to leave for other cites or to go back to Antioch, he looked for people mature enough to be given the charge to watch over the newly formed churches. For example, at the end of his first trip, when he returned with Barnabas to Lystra, Iconium, and Pisidian Antioch, they strengthened the disciples they had made the first time they had been there and "appointed elders for them in each church" (Acts 14:23).

Apostolic Centers

Sixth, in certain cities like Corinth and Ephesus, Paul took residence for up to three years and led the churches through the initial stages, developing them into apostolic centers that went on to have influence over large provinces.

Apostolic Networks

Seventh, all those churches and apostolic centers were linked into relational networks that Paul kept feeding by either visiting them, sending team members, or writing letters (remember that in those days, a letter was a very precious piece of communication).

Bottom Line

In summary, what we see in the second part of the Book of Acts is how apostolic centers were developed into true bases of operation for the apostles and their teams, who then went out and founded communities of believers all around the world. These new communities stayed connected through organic networks and had a tremendous impact on society, releasing a great power for transformation.

Why should it be any different in the church today?

TWO TYPES OF GOVERNMENT

The traditional picture we have today for the government of the local church is either a board of elders (or deacons) leading the congregation and having authority over the pastor, or it is a senior pastor functioning as the main leader of the congregation, balanced by a board of elders (or deacons) that ensures he is not using his authority incorrectly. Now, this is of course oversimplified, but at the same time I can easily imagine many of you nodding with a smile. But is this model in line with what we see in Acts? Let's take a look at eldership.

Elders in Acts

A good place to start is Acts 20. Paul had been in Ephesus for three years (see Acts 20:31) when a crisis situation forced him to leave abruptly; he quickly gathered the disciples, said good-by, and left for Greece (see Acts 20:1–2). He spent the winter in Corinth and then started to travel again. When he passed by Miletus, he asked the elders of Ephesus to come and meet with him. Ephesus was about 30 to 50 kilometers away, but the elders hadn't seen Paul for about a year and gladly made the trip. The time they spent with Paul is reported in verses 18–38.

A good question to ask is: *When were these elders appointed?* From Acts 14:23, we see Paul and Barnabas, two apostles, appointed elders in churches they had founded. Elders were not elected by the congregation; they were appointed by apostles. So, Paul could have appointed elders in Ephesus too, but it's not recorded. When he left for Greece, it was the disciples he gathered—there is no mention of elders (see Acts 20:1–2). If they were already in place, was Paul in too much of a hurry to call for an official elders meeting at the last minute? We don't know. But what is sure is that when he came back a year later, there were elders.

A possibility is that, before joining Paul in Greece, Timothy, who could have been just back from Macedonia (see Acts 19:22), had stayed in Ephesus for a few months and had appointed the elders himself. Some Bible commentators believe this is what the first letter to Timothy is referring to when Paul wrote, "As I urged you when I went into Macedonia, stay there in Ephesus" (1 Tim 1:3), and then gave him instructions concerning appointing elders. Most of the commentators, though, are of the persuasion that this letter was written later, after Paul's first imprisonment in Rome, in which case it would have been additional elders whom Timothy appointed at the time of the letter.

Continuing on the subject of when elders were appointed in the early church, we can also mention what Paul wrote to Titus: "The reason I left you in Crete was that you might straighten out what was left unfinished and appoint elders in every town, as I directed you" (Titus 1:5). We end up with historical evidence that in some churches elders were appointed very early on, while in other churches it was a matter of years before that happened. And in other churches, like in Corinth, elders are never even mentioned, though the disciples there were exhorted to submit to the household of Stephanas, who was possibly an elder.

What factors determined whether the elders would be appointed at the beginning or later? I see mainly one: whether the founding apostle was staying or leaving. This point is important. We'll come back to this shortly.

Elders, Overseers, Pastors

Let's first return to Paul's last visit in Ephesus. In Acts 20:17, Paul asked for the *elders* of the church, and when they arrived, he called them *overseers* and told them they had been chosen to *shepherd* the church:

> Keep watch over yourselves and all the flock of which the Holy Spirit has made you overseers. Be shepherds of the church of God, which he bought with his own blood (Acts 20:28).

So, the terms *elders* and *overseers* are interchangeable and refer to those who have been appointed by the Holy Spirit to shepherd (or pastor) the church. What did the mandate of the elders to shepherd the church involve? Mainly three things: steward the work that had been established, feed the flock, and protect the believers from the enemy. This pastoral mandate was to be carried out in strict agreement with the foundational teachings and instructions that were given by the apostles. Here are some examples:

I know that after I leave, savage wolves will come in among you and will not spare the flock. Even from your own number men will arise and distort the truth in order to draw away disciples after them. So be on your guard! Remember that for three years I never stopped warning each of you night and day with tears (Acts 20:29–31).

An elder must be blameless...Since an overseer manages God's household...he must hold firmly to the trustworthy message as it has been taught, so that he can encourage others by sound doctrine and refute those who oppose it (Titus 1:6–9).

To the elders among you...be shepherds of God's flock that is under your care, watching over them—not because you must, but because you are willing, as God wants you to be; not pursuing dishonest gain, but eager to serve; not lording it over those entrusted to you, but being examples to the flock (1 Pet. 5:1–3).

Nowhere do we see elders or pastors either planting new churches or leading existing churches into major developments. This mandate belonged to apostles working with apostolic teams. Pastors are appointed to steward, care, and protect; apostles are sent to invade, occupy, and transform.

Pastoral Churches

Whenever Paul was founding a new church, it is clear that as long as he stayed at the church with his team, there was no question as to who was leading. The apostle was in charge. It was only when he was about to leave that he would appoint elders or pastors to take care of the work that had been established. In those cases, the church passed from the initial apostolic founding stage to an eldership government, meaning it was now led by a team of elders or pastors. I call this model the *pastoral church*.

Most of the churches Paul founded were pastoral churches or, as we commonly call them today, *local churches*. But contrary to the traditional picture we are used to seeing today, those churches remained aligned with the apostle, who kept contact with them through members of his mobile team, letters, or occasional visits. In some cases, Paul would send one of the apostles he had trained to go and work for a season with the elders of a church and put a few things in order. Titus in Crete is a good example of this, as well as Timothy in Ephesus.

What I'm saying here is that the plan for pastoral churches was to stay in healthy alignment with the apostolic direction. Unfortunately, over the centuries, as the apostolic ministry disappeared from the common church grid, we have ended up with a church system that only has a fraction of the transformation power it was intended to have. This is not to say that we don't find extraordinary pastors in today's traditional local churches but that the old wineskin that has prevailed up to now has not been conducive to reaching our full original potential. This is why the reformation we talk about in this book is so needed for the traditional local churches, either for their transformation into apostolic centers or their alignment with twenty-first century apostolic networks.

Apostolic Centers

While the number of pastoral churches kept increasing everywhere, in some cities Paul settled down and stayed. He became a residing apostle and assumed direct leadership long enough to develop another type of church, a church with an apostolic government and structure. In those cases, the government of the church was not made up of elders but instead a multi-gifted apostolic team led by an apostle. I call this model the *apostolic center.*

Corinth and Ephesus are two good examples of apostolic centers; building from the example of Antioch, Paul established them as resource centers for their entire provinces. For example, from the base he developed in Ephesus, Paul was able to reach all Asia: "All the Jews and Greeks who lived in the province of Asia heard the word of the Lord" (Acts 19:10). This was further confirmed by a silversmith named Demetrius, who complained that his idolatrous business was at risk of a losing income due to Paul's influence "in practically the whole province of Asia" (Acts 19:24–26). God also did extraordinary miracles through Paul in Ephesus; illnesses were cured and evil spirits left people (see Acts 19:11–12). The spiritual activity released from that apostolic center led to a transformation in the lifestyle of large segments of the population, who made public confessions and burned great piles of books on witchcraft (see Acts 19:18–19).

Corinth, where Paul had spent a year and a half, had a central role in the province of Achaia. When Paul greeted the church in 2 Corinthians 1:1, he also greeted "all his holy people throughout Achaia." When he asked the church of Corinth to give an offering for the needs of their brothers in Judea, he positioned them as the representatives for the province of Achaia (see 2 Cor. 9:2).

Apostolic centers had a visibility and impact that made them stand out in the spiritual landscape. An apostolic anointing flowed from them that generated multiple missions, with teams coming in and going out for the business of the kingdom of God, like Timothy and Erastus, who were sent from Ephesus to Macedonia (see Acts 19:22).

Government and Growth

I know I mentioned two types of church government, but it would be more accurate to say there were two variations of the same governmental model. Truly, in both cases, the leadership was exercised by the apostle—in a direct way for the apostolic centers and from a distance or through intermediaries for the pastoral churches.

One last thing. Even in the cases where elders were given the responsibility to take care of the church (in the absence of a residing apostle), it is never suggested that a maintenance mode had become acceptable for the church. On the contrary, churches that have proper alignment with an apostle should experience growth, change, and development. If not, they are operating contrary to the Great Commission, which is apostolic in nature and must continually lead to new developments. There is a big difference between guarding the godly deposit the apostles have laid and falling into a maintenance mode. We did not receive to keep but to give away.

MAINTENANCE VS. DEVELOPMENT

As we study Paul, we see that one thing he consistently did was develop other leaders. The example of Timothy is well known, Timothy being one of the many whom Paul sent on numerous missions. That principle of developing others was then passed on to Timothy so that he could do the same and then find men who, in turn, would also develop others:

> And the things you have heard me say in the presence of many witnesses entrust to reliable men who will also be qualified to teach others (2 Tim. 2:2).

That's probably one of the most important distinctions between a traditional local church and an apostolic center. In the local church, the pastor ministers to the people; in the apostolic center, the apostle works with his team to *equip the saints to do the ministry* (see Eph. 4:11–12).

You see, the apostolic mindset is constantly turned toward the future, toward development; the pastoral mindset is more geared toward the ongoing well-being of the flock. That, of course, is not a bad thing in and of itself, as long as pastoral leaders stay connected with apostolic leaders who will help them to not lose sight of the long-term vision while using their nourishment gifts. As for apostles, they need to include a solid pastoral component in their team because pastoring is an area in which they are typically weak, and they would be the first to admit it. Both types of churches have their place; they each express a different emphasis of the global mandate of the church and need to be in relationship with one another.

At this time, I think it would be helpful to give some of the main characteristics of modern-day apostolic centers. This is by no means an exhaustive list, but it will help us paint a clearer picture of what we are talking about and help differentiate apostolic centers from traditional local churches. I found Peter Wagner's document titled "Apostolic Centers" to be very helpful, as he included in the article many of the characteristics I will mention. He first released that document in a session he led at Glory of Zion's *Head of the Year* conference on September 21, 2012. I want to thank him for his excellent work, which facilitated mine.

APOSTOLIC CENTERS

I have already mentioned that the focus in apostolic centers is on training people to do the ministry rather than on ministering to them. People are thus treated as disciples rather than simply as converts. They are not trained to fit the church programs but to fulfill their destiny. The difference is quite important; while converts are flocking *into* local churches, apostolic centers aim to send disciples *out* as soon as possible; apostolic centers are springboards for the saints!

All this is a direct result of the governmental gift of the apostle who is leading the apostolic center. It's not that he doesn't care for the sheep; he does! But his vision is to mobilize an army to invade, occupy, and transform. He thinks kingdom before congregation, and that's why apostolic centers do well to have good pastors on the team to tend the flock while the apostle is constantly strategizing new ways to move forward.

In apostolic centers, people are trained to be ambassadors of the kingdom on all seven mountains of influence in society, not just on the mountain of religion. To that effect, apostolic centers are not a fellowship club but a legislative assembly with authority to enforce heaven's decrees on the earth.

With that, a real culture of creativity, entrepreneurship, and risk-taking is encouraged. There is an atmosphere of freedom and exuberance, which translates into passionate throne room worship, joyful living, and powerful prayers of proclamation; apostolic centers are a nightmare for the devil! They are always on the offensive, attacking the fortresses of the enemy with shouts of praise!

If you compare the governmental structure of an apostolic center with that of a local church, you can see they are quite different. In an apostolic center, the apostle is the leader. He is not an employee and, consequently, he cannot be fired. He surrounds himself with an apostolic team to help him move things forward. In this team, there are a variety of ministry gifts. And if elders are included in the structure, they are there to support the apostle, not to watch him. Does this mean he is not accountable to anyone? No, apostles are accountable to other apostles. Since the beginning of the New Apostolic Reformation, more and more apostles have been recognized, and numerous apostolic networks have been established, providing a healthy accountability structure. Apostles are not self-appointed; they are commissioned by other apostles.

What about the finances? I'm sure you have already figured out that apostolic centers don't do very well with the spirit of poverty. They believe in extravagant giving and in miraculous access to heavenly resources, and funds are typically not kept for maintenance but instead are happily spent on outreach.

Lastly, while local churches are often part of a denomination, apostolic centers are usually aligned with an apostolic network, which is first and foremost a relational structure rather than a legal one. In fact, it's not uncommon to see a new apostolic network develop around an apostolic center.

Now, this gives us a better understanding of what apostolic centers are, but it still doesn't answer every question. Let's pretend, just for a moment, that we had lots of time for dialogue, and after our discussions, I prepared a list of FAQs (Frequently Asked Questions). Here's what it could look like:

FAQ: APOSTOLIC CENTERS

1. **Do we believe in the church?**
   Absolutely! Jesus said, "… I will build my church, and the gates of Hades will not overcome it" (Matt. 16:18). And in Acts 2:47 we read, "… and the Lord added to their number [to the church] daily those who were being saved."

2. **Why do we use the term *apostolic center*?**
   First, I want to clarify that an apostolic center is a church. For those who are part of an apostolic center, it is their local church. The term *apostolic center* is useful to identify a type of church, whereas when we use the traditional term *local church,* the image that immediately comes to mind is of a pastoral church.

3. **Why not simply say an *apostolic church* instead of *apostolic center*?**
   The church of Jesus Christ is apostolic by nature. So, if we talk about the apostolic church, we should include *all* types of churches. The term *apostolic center* is useful to identify a particular type of church that is directly led by an apostle.

4. Will apostolic centers replace local churches?

Local church is the traditional term we use for a more pastoral type of church. Some of these traditional local churches will go through a transformation to become apostolic centers, but certainly not all of them. Both types of churches are necessary. One doesn't take the place of the other, no more than apostles can replace pastors. The different types of churches, just like different types of ministries, work together, completing one another.

5. Is the apostolic center superior to the local church?

It's in a spirit of humility and service that the diverse parts of the body of Christ function. There is only one church, manifested in various ways. Apostolic centers are one of the expressions of the church of Jesus Christ to serve the kingdom of God. An apostolic center is a church that is the operational base of an apostle, and for its members, it is also a local church. The traditional local church is more of the pastoral type, which doesn't stop it from having some apostolic or prophetic aspects as well. It's not a question of superiority but of diversity of ministries in mutual respect.

LE CHEMIN CROSSING OVER

When we started to track down the apostolic beginnings in the Scriptures, we were a semi-thriving church with a fresh vision, certainly not in a maintenance mode, but hindered by an old wineskin. For close to two years, we studied and prepared for transforming from a local church into an apostolic center. Up to that point, we had been following an apostolic model to a certain degree, but without the full clarity that was now coming to us regarding this new wineskin. I had been functioning as a senior pastor with the authority of an apostle, surrounded by a supportive team of elders, in a paradigm between the old and the new.

It was really the discovery of Antioch that was a great eye-opener for me. We had been looking for landmarks, and with Paul's journeys, they were finally coming alive. At the end of the second year, we left the eldership model, and I established an apostolic team to help me lead Le Chemin, now officially an apostolic center. In the next chapter, you're going to see how we did it and how you can do it too!

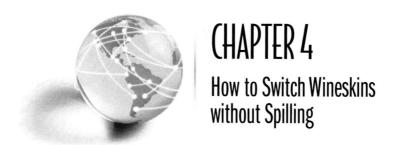

CHAPTER 4

How to Switch Wineskins without Spilling

ASSESS YOUR FOUNDATIONS

Each church has a history (unless you're just starting); work with it. When we want to make any shift, especially a radical one, it's always wise to find points of continuity that can link our future to our past. There might not be very many, but even just a few is better than none. So, making a true evaluation of where we stand will help us to progress without unnecessary stumbling.

One thing I am discovering is that there are cycles in life, whether we are talking about nature, people, economics, or even organizations. The Bible, for example, records how God ordered feasts around agricultural harvest cycles to give us insight and connection with the cycles of the spiritual life, like the successions of seasons of sowing and reaping. The progressive revelation of Jesus unfolded according to the pattern of those feasts. It's worthwhile to be attentive to the cycles around us and especially to those that are directly affecting us.

At Le Chemin, we discovered that we have a twelve-year cycle for our spiritual seasons. The church was founded in 1975. Twelve years later, in 1987, I met the Lord in that church. Now, that was not significant just because of me, but there was a wave of salvation of young adults that year and a fresh breeze that blew on the church. Twelve years later, in 1999, I became the lead pastor, and that of course brought a new style and a different season. Then twelve years after that, in 2011, we made the transition to an apostolic center.

Each change of cycle could have been a breaking point, but instead we continued to develop without division or fracture. I believe the key was the healthy set of values Jean-Claude and Valerie implemented from the beginning. Then when I became the pastor, I made sure to move in continuity with those values, and in the same way, when we came to the apostolic shift, the same values again kept us moving together. What are those values, you may ask? Well, among the main ones are non-negotiable love, thirst and hunger for the presence of God, and living as a family in the church. I will never forget some of Pastor Jean-Claude's famous sentences: "I want to go back to my first love"; "I yield all control to the Holy Spirit"; "Here at the chapel, we do things together."

So, by all means, assure continuity by building on the strengths of the foundation and in sync with the divine cycles that are in operation in your midst. And if you happen to find some cracks in the foundation, it would be prudent to first take time to repair those breaches before going any farther. There might be some reconciliation issues that need to be taken care of or some doctrinal positions to bring adjustment to. Whatever the case may be, there's no point building on a cracked foundation, and there's no gain in moving ahead of God's timing.

Things don't happen overnight. They grow into existence according to the seed principle. We all come from somewhere, and we need to understand where we've been if we want to make the right steps toward accomplishing what we see on the horizon. The most fruitful suddenlies are always those that have been the most carefully prepared!

CHANGING A CHURCH MINDSET IN TWO YEARS

Process

Some of the leaders reading this book might start to realize that in reality their approach is more apostolic than pastoral, and that could explain why they have never felt totally released in the context of the church they have been operating in for a number of years. Perhaps they are finding a new hope at the possibility of shifting from their traditional setting to an apostolic center. Can I speak one word of guidance? *Process.*

Whenever we receive a new vision, we must realize the people around us are not in our heads to see what we see at the same time we see it! Sometimes we may forget that—especially if we are visionary leaders.

Strong visionaries tend to focus so much on what they see that they become oblivious to the reality of the people surrounding them and to the steps needed to reach their goal. Anything that stands between now and their preferred future is viewed as cumbersome. I know the feeling. But if we don't discipline ourselves to enjoy the journey as much as the destination, we risk discovering that we're all alone when we finally cross the finish line, having lost everyone else along the way.

That is why it is imperative to pace ourselves and to gradually disclose the revelation we want to pass on. Visions need to be broken down into bite-sized pieces and be presented consistently, one bite at the time.

Switching wineskins without spilling requires careful steps. The first thing to do is to lay down the proper scriptural foundation. No big bang on a Sunday morning to an unprepared congregation; we want saints journeying with the Holy Spirit, not congregants who are shocked by a sudden change in direction.

For a transition to happen harmoniously, a rhythm needs to be respected. Jacob's response to his brother Esau, who wanted him to move on quickly, is full of wisdom for us:

But Jacob said to him, "My lord knows that the children are tender and that I must care for the ewes and cows that are nursing their young. If they are driven hard just one day, all the animals will die. So let my lord go on ahead of his servant, while I move along slowly at the pace of the droves before me and that of the children, until I come to my lord in Seir" (Gen. 33:13–14).

Case Study

This chapter is a case study to help others make the same transition we did. I thought it would be helpful to present the main points I taught on Sunday mornings during the two years of the transition. The first year was the preparation; the second, the shift. I systematically used the Sunday platform to instill vision and build momentum, while delegating the pastoral care to cell leaders and pastors during the week. Altogether, two years of focused visionary teaching changed our general mindset and made us ready to embrace our apostolic destiny.

You will see that I never put any emphasis on the office of the apostle itself. I didn't find it necessary. I focused instead on the apostolic nature of the church, which led us to reconsider our corporate structure and mandate. When I saw we were headed in the direction of an apostolic center, it was quite obvious that if this concept and model were to be embraced by all, the recognition of the office of the apostle wouldn't be very far down the road.

Also, keep in mind that I was myself discovering the path week after week, desiring to see the church become a better and healthier community, filled with God's glory, and fit to impact and transform the world around us.

The next few pages will give you a snapshot of our process as a whole, from a Sunday pulpit series perspective, as well as an annotated diary of the main steps taken in 2011, the year of the actual shift. I am not suggesting you take the order of those topics and steps as a plan to follow. If I could go back, there's a lot I would change. But it will be helpful to show a *process* and a *progression*, and that's what I want you to see.

YEAR 1: THE PREPARATION
Summary from the Pulpit for 2010

A Community Aligned with Heaven
- We need to preach and demonstrate the kingdom: "As you go, preach this message: 'The kingdom of heaven is near.' Heal the sick, raise the dead, cleanse those who have leprosy, drive out demons. Freely you have received; freely give" (Matt.10:7-8).
- We need to become the church Jesus dreams of, according to the vision Jacob had: the house of God and the gate of heaven (see Gen. 28:17).
- We need to be heaven's penetration point on earth, the headquarters of the kingdom of heaven on earth.
- We need to continue the work of Jesus Christ to bring the model from heaven on earth, like Moses did as a type: "See to it that you make everything according to the pattern shown you on the mountain" (Heb. 8:5).
- We are a kingdom community aligned with heaven.
- We are a community that proclaims and acts.
- We are a community that opens the gates of heaven and shuts the gates of hell.

A Community Aligned with Its Roots
- Let's go back to our first mission—back to the Acts model.
- Peter announced the beginning of a new era with signs and wonders that will last until the Lord returns (see Acts 2:16-20).
- He promised great revivals (see Acts 2:21).
- What's the message?
  - o Jesus is risen; He went up to heaven and sent the Holy Spirit.
  - o Repent and become disciples of Jesus by being baptized.

    o Form a new community on the earth, a community filled with
      the Holy Spirit.
- What was this new community? It is our base model.

The Base Model

Those who accepted his message were baptized, and about three thousand
were added to their number that day. They devoted themselves to the apostles'
teaching and to the fellowship, to the breaking of bread and to prayer.
Everyone was filled with awe, and many wonders and miraculous signs were
done by the apostles. All the believers were together and had everything in
common. Selling their possessions and goods, they gave to anyone as he had
need. Every day they continued to meet together in the temple courts. They
broke bread in their homes and ate together with glad and sincere hearts,
praising God and enjoying the favor of all the people. And the Lord added to
their number daily those who were being saved (Acts 2:41–47).

YEAR 2: THE SHIFT
Summary from the Pulpit for 2011 and Major Steps Taken

January 9, Sunday Message: "In 2011—Back to Acts"

(In this opening Sunday message for the year 2011, I made the
declaration, "We want to become an apostolic base like Antioch." This
became a theme we continued to explore Sunday after Sunday.)
- Acts 2:41–47 was the beginning. Let's see the evolution with Paul
  and Antioch.
- The church of Jerusalem went on with signs and wonders, with
  miracles and healings, to the extent that even those waiting at
  tables were doing miracles: "Now Stephen, a man full of God's
  grace and power, performed great wonders and signs among the
  people" (Acts 6:8).
- Reactions and accusations caused Stephen to be stoned.
- This led to Paul (Saul) (see Acts 7:58–8:3) and his conversion
  (see Acts 9:1–6).

Antioch

- The church grew and spread as the disciples fled Jerusalem because of the persecution. Soon *another center developed: Antioch.*
- Barnabas went to get Paul in Tarsus. Together they strengthened the church at Antioch, where the name *Christians* was used for the first time (see Acts 11:25–26).

Paul and the Church of Antioch Now on the Forefront

- Acts 13:1–4: They were sent by the Holy Spirit but accountable to the church. After a three-year trip, they returned to Antioch and reported to the church.
- Paul established churches in the known world, and *Antioch was the base* for that apostolic ministry.

In 2011, We Want To Be Like Antioch: A Base for the Apostolic Spirit That Was on Paul

- The example of his first trip after the church at Antioch laid hands on him and Barnabas (see Acts 13–14):
  o A team
  o Many cities
  o Made disciples in the midst of opposition
  o Left the cities with new communities established
  o Revisited those cities on their way back (see Acts 14:21–22)
  o Returned to Antioch and reported

Le Chemin—Like Antioch, an Apostolic Base

- We are called to be an operational hub—a center that radiates.
- Internally, we are a community like Acts 2; externally, a church like Antioch.
- We are a church that trains men, women, and youth for ministries that are inside and outside the church.

- We are a church that strengthens existing churches and establishes new ones.
- We are a center where the Holy Spirit continually fills His disciples and gives them missions.
- We need to see ourselves in this way! Put ourselves in the Bible; that's our history we read there!

January 23, Sunday Message: "Finances"

- The apostolic church that advances the kingdom of God on the earth until Jesus comes back must have a clear understanding of the financial principles of the kingdom.

February 27, Sunday Message: "A Church of Leaders"

- In the apostolic church, God wants leaders.
- Paul built apostolic teams that changed the world.

March 6, Sunday Message: "A Heart to Hear"

- In the end-times, God is preparing this apostolic church we see in Acts:
  - A church that will walk with authority on the earth
  - A church entirely devoted to God, listening and obeying His voice

May 8, Sunday Message: "A Roof for Haiti"

- Stirring ourselves to love and good works—raising funds to put a roof on a church affected by the 2010 catastrophic earthquake in Haiti.
- The end-times apostolic church takes care of the people of God.
- This led to a historic $32,000 revival offering on October 9, Thanksgiving Sunday, in a congregation of about 150 people. You can read that whole story in Chapter 6.

June 4: Creation of an Extended Leadership

I put together a list of people I called "extended leadership" and asked them to answer two questions for June 20. Here's an excerpt of the original email I sent them:

This email is sent to an "extended leadership" of about fifty people. Not all are leaders with a position, but for sure everyone has leadership potential. It does not constitute a closed group and does not give a title either. It just represents a sample of all the remarkable and excellent people forming the house of God. I would like to meet with you before the summer starts. Could you answer two questions?

1. What are the *strengths* of our church? (What are we doing well? What defines us, strikes us as a success, that we notice when we come to this church that makes us proud before God, etc.)
2. What are the *weaknesses* of our church? (What are we doing with less success, what are we not doing, what are we not able to do, what is missing as a church, etc.)

If it is possible for you, send me your response by email in the next couple days. You could also add whatever the Lord has been speaking to you about the church. We will talk about it a little on June 20, and we will then be able to continue this reflection during the summer. I'll be waiting for your input, and I'll see you soon.

Oh, I almost forgot! This week, I planted my garden. I am confident a harvest is in the making!

June 20: First Extended Leadership Meeting

This started a series that is still going strong on the first Monday night of each month. It's a key meeting to communicate and refresh vision, see where we're at as an apostolic center, check to see how the cell groups are doing, and teach leadership principles to develop our skills. It brings together active leaders—pastors, leaders, cell leaders, and assistants, as well as potential future leaders. During the apostolic shift, the extended leadership was the final circle I would always explain our next step to and build agreement with just before I would speak to the congregation.

September and October: Preparing Key Leaders
I held Individual meetings with three categories of people:
- Existing elders: letting them know that the eldership model would be dismantled before the end of the year and replaced by an apostolic team. Discussed with them their future role or position. Some were considered for the apostolic team; others were not.
- Potential members for the apostolic team.
- Potential members for the vision and direction team: a smaller team taken from the larger apostolic team to help Marie and me lead the apostolic center.

September 4, Sunday Message: "A New Society for the End-Times"
- "Save yourselves from this corrupt generation" (Acts 2:40), i.e. form a new society in the world, a society within the society.
- We are to be a society that lives according to Acts 2:42–47, with the four pillars of the church being the study of the Bible, fellowship, worship and prayer, and communion.
- The result of that society is a lifestyle where "everyone was filled with awe, and many wonders and miraculous signs were done" (Acts 2:43).
- With the level of God's presence rising, the fear of God needs to rise as well—signs and wonders.
- The key for the end-times is the community of the children of God living together in the world.
- Ministries will only be great in the context of a people living together.
- We are to be a vehicle on the earth to God's glory, a distinct society and agents of change.
- Our cell groups are hot spots for the kingdom in the city.

October 23, Sunday Message: "Apostolic Transition"

In this pivotal message, I announced that a new structure would be established in December. An apostolic team would replace the existing elders. We thanked and honored them all for their labor of love and faithfulness through the years.

Review
- We are called to be an apostolic church according to the model of Antioch.
- We receive God's life and give God's life.

A New Cycle for Our Church
- As a church, we're entering the adult stage.
- We're not fully mature yet, but responsible.

The Church in Quebec:
- We have received, but will now give.
- We were poor, but will now enrich others.
- We lived in a survival mode, but will now live.
- We were barren, but will now rejoice and give birth.
- We were on the defensive, but will now go on the offensive.
- We were bound by fear, but will now advance with courage.
- We were living in shame, but will now lift our head up.

A New Structure (New Wineskin)
- In the New Testament, two government structures existed: apostolic teams and councils of elders.
- The apostolic teams developed, established the kingdom, preached, proclaimed, and eventually appointed elders to keep and watch, *but* not while the apostolic team was there—only when it left.
- We are not in a maintenance mode but in a development mode.
- We are returning to the apostolic structure that will replace the

eldership model.
- We thank the elders because they have done their work well.
- In December, I will establish the apostolic team with a new operational mode for the church to move forward.
- A smaller team inside the apostolic team will help Marie and I give vision and direction.

The Apostolic Church
- The church is apostolic by nature.
- The history of the church is the Holy Spirit leading an apostolic community.
- Ephesians 2:20 lists a company of apostles and prophets (plural) with Jesus (alone) as the cornerstone.
- Hebrews 3:1—Jesus is our apostle.
- *Apostolos* (noun) and *apostello* (verb) mean, "The leader of a fleet sent with the king's authority to invade, conquer, and occupy a country in his name."
- We are replacing the tyrant and his kingdom with the kingdom and culture of our King.
- Jesus came down from heaven, from another kingdom, and established an apostolic team around him. He started to invade this kingdom to make Satan's throne fall, to bring a new law of liberty to the captives.
- Jesus gave this same mission to the church, and that's why the church is apostolic.
- "As you sent [*apostello*] me into the world, I have sent [*apostello*] them into the world" (John 17:18).

Jesus' Apostolic Mission in Luke 4:18-19
The Spirit of the Lord is on me, because he has anointed me to proclaim good news to the poor. He has sent [*apostello*] me to proclaim freedom for the prisoners and recovery of sight for the blind, to set the oppressed free [*apostello*], to proclaim the year of the Lord's favor.

- The Spirit of God sets the captives free and makes of them apostles; He *apostello* them out of prison and sends them to preach and make darkness crumble.
- Our mission is to go because we have been sent (*apostello*) to announce freedom to the captives, telling them to repent because they have adopted the ways of the tyrant and his lies. But now a new king is here: Come and bow before Him, and He will forgive. He is a merciful King.
- We are in a new dimension with His authority. We are ready to answer the King's call. Morning has broken, a new day has dawned, the stone's been rolled away, and we have risen with Him to reign.

October 23: First Official Vision and Direction Meeting

This meeting took place in the afternoon after the Sunday gathering. It brought together six couples, including Marie and me and our founding pastors, Jean-Claude and Valerie.

October 30, Sunday Message: "The Apostolic Room"

- The secret place is the key for apostolic authority and power (see Matt. 6:6).

November 6, Sunday Message: "Transform the City: Activate the Company of the Prophets"

- The prophetic company walks alongside the apostolic direction (see Ezra 5:1–2; Eph. 2:20).
- The end-times church is not only apostolic but also prophetic; the very first thing the apostle Peter preached at the birth of the church (the very first time the apostolic ministry started to function in the church), was regarding restoring the prophetic ministry for the end-times; this is why it's written that the church is built on the foundation of the apostles and prophets.
- If we want to touch the city, the church needs to be both apostolic and prophetic.

November 10: Email to Vision and Direction Team

I gave them the list of the fifteen people/couples I had chosen for the apostolic team. Here's an excerpt:

> Here's the list of people I have in mind for the apostolic team (which includes people with diverse gifts and ministries, as well as the six couples from the vision and direction team). I'm ready to send them an invitation for November 27. I'll also meet with them individually to explain everything and tell them about the six couples chosen for vision and direction.

November 13: Email to Future Apostolic Team

Here's an excerpt of what I sent to the apostolic team I chose:

> I would like to invite you to stay for lunch after the service on Sunday, November 27. We've talked for several months about forming an apostolic team that will walk in the ways of the Lord to bring His church where He wants it to go. On November 27, I would like to establish this team, and *I'm inviting you to be a part of it.* It will initially be composed of about fifteen people/ couples, having varied gifts and ministries, but all having an apostolic dimension in their callings. This team will not have a rigid structure but will remain flexible to adapt to the movement of the Holy Spirit. The team will, therefore, evolve in composition, form, and function while following the spiritual seasons.
>
> I will do my best to meet with you individually before November 27 to talk in more detail and to be able to share together. I also want to note that when an invitation is given to a person it also always includes that person's spouse; this has been the way the Lord has led us to function in our church.

November 20, Sunday Message: "Transform the City: Activate the Company of the Evangelists"

- Evangelists in the end-times function like John with the prophetic spirit, under the apostolic mission of Jesus.

November 20: Vision and Direction Lunch
This lunch was a strategy meeting for the transition, held after the Sunday gathering.

November 27, Sunday Message: "Transform the City: Activate the Company of the Intercessors"
- We have conceived in the apostolic chamber.
- We have established the apostolic foundation.
- We have activated the prophets.
- We have activated the evangelists.
- This morning the Lord is activating the intercessors; it's time to give birth.

November 27: Apostolic Team
We held a meeting to establish the apostolic team after the Sunday gathering, in an intimate setting.

December 18, Sunday Message: "The Glory of Acts"
This was the closing message of the year, proclaiming that the Lord wanted to establish an apostolic base. I ended the meeting with the official presentation of the apostolic team to the congregation.
- This concludes our *Back to Acts* year.
- We have seen that the strength of the Book of Acts was an apostolic company led by the Holy Spirit; Acts 1:8 is the key.
- As Mary was visited by the cloud of glory (*episkiazzo*), the same glorious cloud that came at the transfiguration, the church was covered by the glory at Pentecost.
- The apostolic team I'm presenting today is soaking in this glory that's upon us.
- It's a mobile, flexible team, led by the Holy Spirit—compared to the old model, where each leader was in his own a box in a fixed

position.
- With the apostolic base we have established, we will see the expansion of the kingdom of God everywhere we go in 2012.
- Allow the Lord to stretch your minds beyond the models we have seen before because we are a people born under the cloud of glory at Pentecost, and we continue to live under it; we are partakers of God's glory on earth.
- When His glory comes down, it's on us, His church.

Presentation of the Apostolic Team
- This team will help Marie and I lead this church.
- Jean-Claude and Valerie are the apostolic founders of the church, and we go back to our apostolic roots by establishing this apostolic team.
- It will lead the church in its next phase.
- Paul had a few who were closer to him to help him make decisions. In the same way, I chose six couples from the team to help with vision and direction.
- We seal this year by establishing this team.

Prayer
Everlasting Father, we have come to the conclusion of this year, *Back to Acts,* and by returning to Acts, we came back to the apostolic source of a people led by the Holy Spirit, an apostolic company whom You are Yourself leading. Father, we present this team to You this morning...

[To the people]

You have a destiny. It's time to enter into your future. It's time to live your future today. Grab hold of your destiny, in the name of Jesus!

January 8, 2012, Sunday Message: Activation 2012
In my opening message for the year 2012, I said, "In 2011, the church

entered into her maturity. Now as responsible people, let's *activate the Apostolic Center* that God revealed and manifested in 2011."

A NEW WINESKIN FOR A NEW PARADIGM

A paradigm is the way we see the reality we live in. It organizes the world in our heads according to the assumptions and values we adopt, and it traces the path for our vision of the future. Paradigms first belong to the realm of concepts, and then they give birth to structures. For example, if a society has a compassion paradigm, it will create organizations to care for the needs of the people. In the church domain, the understanding we have of our mission will influence the type of governing structures we will put in place. Those structures are what we sometimes call wineskins. Wineskins are thus a reflection of our paradigms. This means that whenever our current paradigm goes through a change, a corresponding adjustment in the life structure will be needed. The wider the paradigm shift is, the more radical the structural change needs to be.

I discovered that as long as we kept the discussion about the apostolic model at a conceptual level, the waters were not too troubled, but as soon as I started going down the path of reforming the church government, a number of insecurities suddenly came to the surface. People don't have a problem with the concept; it's when we touch the structure that we need to be careful. Dismantling a board of elders in order to replace it with an apostolic team is not something I advise any leader to do, anointed or not, without properly walking the congregation and leadership team through progressive steps.

A key to doing this is to honor the previous wineskin and its elders for the work and dedication they have shown over the years, while gradually turning the rudder toward the new direction. There is no use in criticizing the old wineskin; just paint a picture of the new, week after week, by examining the Scriptures until it becomes a clear and attractive model. People will naturally desire to migrate toward that model after a while.

So, I kept presenting an inspiring picture of an apostolic people filled with God's glory on the earth. Drawing from the roots of the early church, I preached a victorious Christian life for today and linked it to an apostolic company of people turning the world upside down. From Sunday to Sunday, I gradually superimposed this picture of an apostolic church on the traditional picture of the local church, and as a result, the new apostolic paradigm gave relatively pain-free birth to a healthy new wineskin that we called an apostolic center.

NO SPILLING

Avoid Casualties and Save Friendships

In order to make the transition from a traditional local church to an apostolic center, the leader needs to either be an apostle or be aligned with an apostle who is ready to be directly involved in the process.

There are two warnings I would give before going farther. First, don't play the apostle if you don't have the calling. There are already too many wannabes, and it's not helping anyone. Seek rather to enter into a healthy alignment with an apostle who will help you flourish in your mandate. Second, if you do have an apostolic calling, don't use your authority in a domineering way. The apostle of the house needs to maintain trust equity with the people. He needs to keep communicating with transparency but without destabilizing the congregation. The house of God is a relational house, and leaders need to be able to win the hearts of their fellow brothers and sisters. The apostolic shift is not to be made by imposing a vision on others or by dictating to the congregation what their lives will become; apostolic authority flows from the Father's tender heart for His people.

Remember, it's not only the goal that counts, but the journey to get there as well. In the pursuit of our visions, we must do all we can to *avoid casualties and save friendships.*

What about the Elders?

Now, what about the elders who lost their position in the shift? I'm sure this is the question you all have at this point in the book. Well, understandably, some tension was felt as a result of that, but not as much as you might think. I walked very carefully with them, sharing my heart and explaining where I was going, taking the time to dialogue both in group settings and in one-on-one meetings. I'll come back to this.

From the Inner Circles to the Outer Ones

There is a simple principle I apply all the time when I want to bring a change in direction. I always start to build agreement with those closer to me before going to the larger body. I move from the inner circle to the outer ones. There are usually a few circles around us, increasing in size as we move out. Try to always secure the support of the closest circle before moving to the next one. My friend Doug Schneider in Oshawa coached me in this, and it has proven to be a very good approach. When those closest to you and, in a leadership context, those with greater influence in the church are in agreement with the changes you want to bring, they are a great help in reassuring the next line of leaders, who in turn do the same to the next circle. And by the time you share with the larger congregation, a spirit of unity is already in place and peace reigns. I've experienced this phenomenon time and time again, and I know for a fact that this is beyond a mechanical result of a good communication strategy; the Lord makes His presence go before you to prepare the way.

Jesus Himself functioned from intimate circles to public ones. There were Peter, James, and John; then the twelve; then the seventy-two; then the larger group of disciples; then the crowds of people. For each circle, He adjusted the level of what He communicated. For example, Mark 4:34 tells us, "He did not say anything to them [the crowd] without using a parable. But when he was alone with his own disciples, he explained everything."

Challenges in Role Recalibration

I started to explain to the closest people around me that the board of elders would be dismantled and would be replaced by an apostolic team that I would choose. That team would be mobile and flexible, and its composition would be subject to change with the spiritual seasons we would go through. Being part of it wouldn't give a fixed position but would need to be the result of a function. In other words, the apostolic team would be different than a board: All its members would need to be active players in the advancement of the apostolic center. From that team, I would choose a smaller group called Vision and Direction to help Marie and me lead wisely and move forward. The apostolic team would have a strong pastoral component, while the vision and direction team would be composed of people with clear apostolic capacity. The two teams ended up being a mosaic of generations, nations, genders, and ministry gifts, not because I tried to have that balance but because that represented the true make-up of our church.

When I met with the elders individually, their reactions were not all the same. For the one who had been in position the longest, for more than twenty-five years, I felt he had done all he could with a good and faithful heart, but with the new era we were in, he should step down completely and join the ranks of the congregation. I wasn't sure what his reaction would be, but I was pleasantly surprised. It was like I had taken a heavy load off his back. He felt so relieved not to have to carry this task any longer in a church setting that was so different from what he had known for years and years. He genuinely rejoiced and felt the Lord was telling him, "Well done, good and faithful servant."

For another elder, I felt he should become part of the apostolic team but not the vision and direction team. This person had been a very close friend to me for many years, and the whole rearrangement was hard for him. It put a strain on our friendship for quite a while. We both suffered and grieved in our hearts, but I knew I had to follow the leading of the Holy Spirit for the new government structure. We met many times and shared our hearts, and eventually, with the passing of time, things fell in place and our friendship survived. Love never fails.

Other elders had questions about the authority structure this would bring and needed a bit of time to absorb the new paradigm, even with the invitation to join the vision and direction team. Again, open communication, study of the Scriptures, prayer, time to process, trust, and the witness of the Holy Spirit brought us all to a place of agreement.

The apostolic team was finally publicly installed in December 2011. I am writing this book eighteen months after that shift, and the team has already grown in number. The most exciting thing for me is to watch how every member has been on a fast development track, especially the six couples on the vision and direction team, who, without exception, are already expanding their action outside the walls of the nuclear congregation as ambassadors of the apostolic center model. Being an apostolic center has generated a high level of enthusiasm in all of us, and the ensuing activity has been remarkable, as we will see later. Now, a little follow-up:

FOLLOW-UP AFTER THE SHIFT

For 2012, the theme I announced was *Activation 2012*, by which I meant, "Let's activate the apostolic center that we just established." In June of that year, we had our first ever apostolic conference, with the theme, "The Apostolic Church Is Rising."

It was to that conference that I invited C. Peter Wagner and met him for the first time. Doug Schneider, himself an apostle aligned with Global Spheres through Peter, had made the first contact for me and was also part of the conference.

I am almost embarrassed to say it, but I had only ever read one book written by Dr. Wagner, back in 1999, titled *Church Quake* (I have now read a few more and have discovered the wealth of Peter's contribution to the body of Christ). When we met, I explained to him the transition we had just been through, and I saw in his reaction that he was greatly interested in our journey. Honestly, I was not really aware we had done anything very special. I had just tried to get back to the model of Acts and then move forward from there. But through his teaching on the apostolic and his comments during the conference, Peter brought another level of clarity and a strong confirmation for the transformation we had completed. This was highly encouraging for us, and I felt we needed to align ourselves with this father and apostle. I will tell you the story of how that happened in the next chapter.

In 2013, the theme I received from the Lord was *The Harvest is Here*. In April, we hosted our second apostolic conference, "Apostolic Centers—The Shift Is Here!" Doug Schneider and C. Peter Wagner were again the speakers, with the addition of Chuck Pierce. At the conference, we started live streaming from our apostolic center, and I launched *HODOS,* a brand new apostolic network. You can visit the website at hodos.ca (English button on the top right).

I'm going to close this chapter by giving you a quick how-to list, and then in the next few chapters, we'll look at the amazing results this transition has brought to us.

HOW-TO LIST

Before You Start
- Keep Jesus the center.
- Desire to give Him the church He longs for.
- Be ready to follow life before structure.
- Refuse the maintenance mode.
- Adopt the kingdom mindset.
- Be ready to switch wineskins.

Assess Your Foundations

- Understand where you've come from before you step forward.
- Know where you stand.
- Find points of continuity to link your future to your past.
- Build on your value system.

Study and Teach the Basics

- Study the base model for a spiritual community in Acts 2.
- Study the Acts 13 shift with the initial apostolic base in Antioch.
- Study the developments with Paul: teams, local churches, centers, networks.

Move from the Inner to the Outer Circles

- Start by building agreement with those closer to you.
- Secure the closest circles before moving to the next ones.
- Try building unity with leaders before going to the larger body.

Move Forward Properly

- Don't rush the journey.
- Disclose the vision gradually, one bite at a time.
- Don't take the congregation by surprise.
- Communicate, communicate, communicate!

Switch Wineskins without Spilling

- Honor the previous wineskin.
- Use Sunday gatherings to instill vision and build momentum.
- Present a clear and attractive model until people naturally desire to migrate.
- Delegate pastoral care to cell leaders or pastors.
- Focus on the apostolic call of the church rather than on the office of the apostle.

- Rally people, win their hearts.
- Don't be a dictator.
- Avoid casualties and save friendships.
- Don't stop halfway.
- Celebrate each step; finish strong.

CHAPTER 5
The Law of Apostolic Attraction

PAUL'S SECRET

I've already mentioned how Paul's sphere kept growing to the point that he had several teams moving simultaneously in different parts of the world. Paul's capacity to mobilize leaders and keep a complex organization flowing, all while facing changing and often challenging circumstances, was undoubtedly remarkable. But what was no less remarkable was his heart and the relational nature of the authority he demonstrated.

This can be seen in the way he addressed the Galatians, "I plead with you, brothers" (Gal. 4:12), and in how vulnerable he made himself when he wrote to the Corinthians:

> We have spoken freely to you, Corinthians, and opened wide our hearts to you. We are not withholding our affection from you, but you are withholding yours from us. As a fair exchange—I speak as to my children—open wide your hearts also (2 Cor. 6:11–13).

This is clearly different from a legal or domineering use of authority. Paul, the apostle, was a true father. Ask the Ephesian elders who "all wept as they embraced him and kissed him" because he had said "that they would never see his face again" (Acts 20:37–38). Or ask Timothy, whom Paul called "my dear son" (2 Tim. 1:2).

But were Paul's amazing strength and heart sufficient to explain the extraordinary pull he had on people? Is this a question of personality alone? There have been other men with great hearts who never really succeeded in gathering leaders around themselves, and there have been some with much less gifted personalities than Paul who have nonetheless been very effective in influencing great companies of men. No, there has to be another factor to add to the equation in order to explain Paul's success in drawing men from everywhere to join his team.

THE LAW OF APOSTOLIC ATTRACTION

At the beginning of my Christian life, I received a prophetic word from an old friend of God named Bob Birch. It was November 29, 1988. He was talking about what my life would become, assuring me that the Lord would give me the grace to discipline myself, place Him first, and walk with Him. I've never forgotten one of the things he told me that day, "He's going to give you companions, associates who will walk with you, and you'll be a strength to others." Little did I know back then that it would be the *law of apostolic attraction* that would allow this prophecy to be fulfilled.

I first saw that law when I was reading about the tense discussion Jesus had with the crowd who found Him in Capernaum the day after He had fed the five thousand. Jesus told them they were only looking for Him because they wanted to eat, but they should instead seek food that endures for eternal life, because He Himself was "the bread that came down from heaven" (John 6:41). At this thought, they started to grumble, and Jesus boldly commanded them to stop, declaring:

No one can come to me unless the Father who sent me draws him... (John 6:44).

In other words, He was telling them He was not there to accommodate their carnal minds with words that would soothe them but to declare the truth unashamedly. His advice to them was to receive that word because it was truly coming from heaven, but since they did not believe, He wanted them to know a higher law was in operation, a law the *Father who sent Him* had put in place, an apostolic law that bypassed their human reasoning and produced an irresistible attraction on men.

Then Jesus, far from making things easier for them, added that if they wanted to receive life, they even needed to eat His flesh and drink His blood (see John 6:53)! Well, many of the disciples just couldn't take that and started to leave. Was Jesus troubled at the sight of all those men walking away from Him? Apparently not. He actually turned to the twelve and asked them if they wanted to leave, too (see John 6:67).

This reaction of Jesus is quite a contrast to the fear that some church leaders have about losing some of their members to another church! Amazingly, Jesus didn't even care to explain to the disciples what He meant by His provocative declarations about drinking His blood and eating His flesh, except that His words were spirit and life (see John 6:63). How about that for a team-building strategy! But He knew that when the apostolic commission operates in a person, the one who gave that commission also activates a law of attraction to bring people to that apostle. This is the same *drawing force* that was released after the victory of Christ on the cross and that continues to operate today:

But I, when I am lifted up from the earth, will draw all people to myself (John 12:32).

All that the Father gives me will come to me... (John 6:37).

As men and women continue to respond to that attraction, they align with Jesus for their personal redemption, and as they do that, they join in the great mission to proclaim and advance the kingdom of God on the earth. *The law of apostolic attraction activates alignment that leads to governmental empowerment.*

That law is one of the greatest forces that operates in apostles today and makes them successful at building strong teams. Apostolic team building is not about recruiting; it's about empowering those who are coming to align as they are prompted to do so by the supernatural attraction.

APOSTOLIC ALIGNMENT

What is apostolic alignment? It is the acknowledgement of a governmental order that God placed in the church. In 1 Corinthians 12:28 we read:

> And God has placed in the church first of all apostles, second prophets, third teachers, then miracles, then gifts of healing, of helping, of guidance, and of different kinds of tongues.

Seeing this not as a hierarchical structure, we prefer to speak of alignment rather than say we are placing ourselves *under* the apostolic covering.

The term *alignment* comes from Ephesians 4:12, "To equip his people for works of service, so that the body of Christ may be built up." The word *equip* comes from the Greek word *katartizo*, which is a medical term meaning to put bones together, hence the concept of aligning the members of the body of Christ.

Alignment breaks the isolation and fragmentation often experienced by the servants of God. There can be several ministries at work in the body of Christ, but if they are not properly aligned, the work is done without unity or an overall plan. The apostles have the ability to unite the members of the body so they can hear and follow the instructions of the Lord in a more cohesive way. When this apostolic alignment is in place, a governmental order can operate and move things forward efficiently.

Joshua would not have become the leader of Israel without aligning with Moses; the group of men who were in distress would not have become mighty men without aligning with David; Timothy, Titus, and Luke—to name just a few—would be unknown to us if they hadn't walked with Paul. Aligning with apostolic authority remains a key to growth and destiny.

Let's look in more detail at how the apostolic attraction that functioned in David's life caused increasing numbers of men to come to him and experience redemptive alignment that eventually qualified them to form the new government over the nation.

FROM A CAVE TO A KINGDOM

Adullam: Apostolic Attraction Causes Redemptive Alignment

David was fleeing for his life. Saul, the king of Israel, had turned mad with jealously and wanted to kill him. He escaped to the cave of Adullam, where his brothers and his father's household joined him. Then about four hundred men arrived: "All those who were in distress or in debt or discontented gathered around him, and he became their leader…" (1 Sam. 22:2). This is apostolic attraction causing alignment, even in the worst circumstances. And it kept growing. By the time they left the refuge of the cave, that odd company had grown to six hundred men (see 1 Sam 23:13).

David's apostolic leadership literally transformed the lives of these men who became the foundation of the army he led all through his long journey from being a fugitive to becoming a king. These men who at first were described as "in distress" became part of a glorious company called "David's Mighty Men." Some of them became chiefs, accomplished extraordinary exploits, and earned the privilege of having their names written in the Bible for the faithful support they gave to David to extend his kingship over the whole land (see 1 Chron. 11:10–47).

Ziklag: The Real Government Lies with the Apostolic Camp

From the cave at Adullam, David and his band moved to the Desert of Ziph, where Saul continued to launch attacks on them. Looking for security, David finally went to the land of the Philistines and was given the city of Ziklag, where he stayed for a year and four months (see 1 Sam. 27:6–7).

Something dramatic happened in Ziklag. During a time when David was away with his six hundred men, a band of Amalekites raided the camp, burned it, and took captive all of the wives, sons, and daughters (see 1 Sam 30:1–3). David didn't waste any time and quickly pursued the enemy, but two hundred of his men were so exhausted that they had to stay behind with the luggage while the rest continued. Victory was won, all the wives and children were delivered, and great spoils were taken.

But when David came back and met up the two hundred who had been too exhausted to follow him, some evil men didn't want to share the plunder with those who had stayed behind. David had to intervene, and he decided that "the share of the man who stayed with the supplies is to be the same as that of him who went down to the battle. All will share alike" (1 Sam. 30:24).

Now, what is completely stunning is the next verse: "David made this a statute and ordinance for Israel from that day to this" (1 Sam. 30:25). Here is a man, living as an outcast with a small band of warriors, making laws for the nation he doesn't know how he will ever go back to, let alone reign over! Yet what David and his apostolic company experienced in their precarious conditions had more influence over the future destiny of the nation they were exiled from than the legal decrees that were made in the capital. *The real government is always exercised from the camp where apostolic alignment is found.*

Exceptional Leaders Attract Exceptional Men

David did not attract only the category of men we saw in Adullam, but many others came to him in Ziklag—drawn by the same apostolic law of attraction: "*Day after day men came* to help David, until he had a great army, like the army of God" (1 Chron. 12:22, emphasis added). But this time, they arrived as powerful and skilled fighters; they were strong, and while the first company portrayed adventurous individuals, the newcomers in Ziklag were identified by the tribe they belonged to, a sign that the governmental authority of David was increasing. The new men were coming to complete the group of mighty men. Take those from the tribe of Gad for example:

> Some Gadites defected to David at his stronghold in the desert. They were brave warriors, ready for battle and able to handle the shield and spear. Their faces were the faces of lions, and they were as swift as gazelles in the mountains (1 Chron. 12:8).

> These Gadites were army commanders; the least was a match for a hundred, and the greatest for a thousand (1 Chron. 12:14).

David's Governmental Courage and Authority

David was able to receive and include new men in his team; he didn't feel threatened or intimidated by strong leaders. When a group of Benjamites and some men from Judah came to David in Ziklag, he went out to meet them and said to them:

> If you have come to me in peace, to help me, I am ready to have you unite with me. But if you have come to betray me to my enemies when my hands are free from violence, may the God of our fathers see it and judge you (1 Chron. 12:17).

At that moment, the Spirit came upon Amasai, chief of the thirty, and he said: "We are yours, O David! We are with you, son of Jesse!" (1 Chron. 12:18), which is equivalent to saying, "We are aligning with you!"

What was David's response? He had in front of him strong leaders asking for alignment. But he didn't know them, at least there's no indication he did. And in his situation, he could not allow himself to make mistakes and open his camp to uncertain forces. But he had witnessed the Spirit come upon their chief, validating his noble declaration. David did what an apostle does when he recognizes that God is in the picture. He not only received them right away, but he even made them leaders of his raiding bands (see 1 Chron. 12:18)!

The same capacity to include new leaders in his team is shown with a group of men who were leaders of units of a thousand in Manasseh. They defected to David, and he made them commanders in his army (see 1 Chron. 12:19–21). David was a man of heart and a man of decision.

Hebron: Apostolic Unity

David stayed in Ziklag until king Saul died. After that, he moved back to Israel and went to live in Hebron. "Then the men of Judah came to Hebron and there they anointed David king over the house of Judah..." (2 Sam. 2:4). He ruled seven years and six months in that city and continued to grow in strength while the old house of Saul grew weaker and weaker. Whole armies from every tribe of Israel kept coming to him by the thousands. In 1 Chronicles 12:38, we read:

> All these were fighting men who volunteered to serve in the ranks. They came to Hebron fully determined to make David king over all Israel. All the rest of the Israelites were also of one mind to make David king.

Then, in verse 40:

> Also, their neighbors from as far away as Issachar, Zebulun and Naphtali came bringing food on donkeys, camels, mules

and oxen. There were plentiful supplies of flour, fig cakes, raisin cakes, wine, oil, cattle and sheep, for there was joy in Israel.

When the right apostolic alignment produces the right government, there's joy in the land, and provisions are released!

Jerusalem: The Kingdom

David went up to Jerusalem, conquered it, took up residence in the fortress, and called it the City of David. He had a palace built for himself and ordered the construction of many houses. But this was not the desire of his heart. He "conferred with his faithful companions, each of his officers, the commanders of thousands and the commanders of hundreds" (1 Chron. 13:1); then he spoke to the whole assembly of Israel and said:

Let us bring the ark of our God back to us, for we did not inquire of it during the reign of Saul (1 Chron. 13:3).

He pitched a tent, placed the ark inside, and turned the heart of the nation back to worship. The ark of the presence became the center of the kingdom. The explanation for the extraordinary attraction David had on men is revealed in that tent: the *holy presence*. This is the key to the law of apostolic attraction. David had surrendered to the pull of that presence from an early age. He had kept his heart in alignment with it every day.

This is what people were feeling around David. This is why they loved him. This is why God was pleased to give him the kingdom.

APOSTLES ATTRACT STRONG LEADERS

When I became the lead pastor of Le Chemin in 1999, the church had about fifty people. In those days, we didn't really talk very much about apostles, although we believed they existed. What happened is that as I started to grow as a leader, my apostolic capacity also developed, and more people started to come. But what was very interesting was the number of people with obvious leadership gifts who were joining us. Some had been leaders in previous churches; others just had the word leadership written all over them.

Leaders are peculiar people. They want to lead. They have strong personalities; some can be in-your-face type people, and even when they are gentle and meek, they still have their own ideas on what direction should be followed and who should lead the way! But there is something else true leaders like: to find another leader they can align with.

Year after year, leaders kept coming, and it was impossible to deny the gifts they carried. Rather than feeling intimidated, I received them with gratefulness and joy. I love the company of leaders. Apostles attract strong leaders and are able to work with them. It is more demanding to lead leaders than to lead followers, but to my appreciation, so much more rewarding.

So I made room for them, found ways to include them in the dealings of the church, and started to ordain many of them. This was before our transition to an apostolic center. Eventually we had quite a large number of pastors for a church of our size, which—even though it was growing—my wife and I probably still could have managed between us. The ratio of ordained ministers to the number of people in the congregation was way over the normal standard. No doubt about that one. But everyone knew somehow this was in God's plan. We sensed we were in preparation for something; the Lord had a reason for bringing so many leaders together in one place, but we didn't know why. The law of apostolic attraction had been activated, but we didn't yet realize it. We were just witnessing its effects.

Then the time of our two-year transition came, and more leaders continued to arrive. And that's without counting the people already in the congregation who started to emerge as leaders too! It has been very interesting. When the apostolic anointing is released in a center, you will see leaders being drawn to it even from remote areas of the nation. I have found no other way to explain why so many leaders, coming from so many different places, continued to walk through our doors and wanted to call this place home. Some arrived in their full strength, ready to work. Others arrived beaten and bleeding, rejected by a religious system that didn't know how to handle them.

I have always been mindful of the family feel within our congregation and desired to see signs of established relationships between the people and the new leaders before giving them public recognition. For a while I first tried to stick to a rule of having new people wait a certain amount of time to integrate before getting involved, but I finally came to the conclusion that every new leader was at a different stage when they arrived, and the time they needed to build healthy relationships with the people varied a lot.

Ultimately, I learned to rely on the guidance of the Holy Spirit on a case-by-case basis regarding the involvement of new people in the team. I have come to realize that someone's past history *in the ministry* does not necessarily announce the truth about his or her future. I'm not saying I don't value the reports given from previous places of ministry, because I do. But at the same time, I have seen a number of leaders come to us bearing the stigma of condemnation, mainly because they did not function well in a wineskin that was too restrictive for their giftings; but take the same people, place them in the wineskin of an apostolic center, and watch them come back to life and cruise again. What a joy!

Let me tell you the stories of a few of my heroes. I happen to have the privilege to count them as companions in the apostolic commission the Lord gave us at Le Chemin. Whether they came at the Adullam stage of their life or joined us at Ziklag or Hebron in their full strength, they all aligned with God's mighty camp and continue to make it stronger. They are all part of our apostolic team.

There are many more leaders I could have mentioned here, and I readily apologize to my friends whom I was not able to include in this list made to fit the format of this book.

MIGHTY WARRIORS AT LE CHEMIN

Pascal and Kyla

Pascal came when he was still a young man. His life with the church had been rocky. Let's just say his personality was a bit rough on the edges, a real in-your-face kind of guy. That didn't facilitate his relationship with previous religious authorities who interpreted his attitude as defiance. Well, they were not completely wrong, but I just loved his heart. What a brilliant and passionate man he was! We had a few confrontations, a number of adjustments; at times the future was uncertain. But our love kept growing, and today Pascal is more than a son to me. He is happily married to Kyla, who is one of the interpreters on Sundays. He was our worship director for a few years, and he now leads the media team, which includes website and live streaming. Seeing the leadership progression in Pascal's life has been a great source of encouragement to me.

Cory and Diana

Cory and Diana came from the west of the country as a young couple, after only having been out of Bible College for a few years. They were both English Canadians, but the Lord had put a desire on their hearts to live among the French people. We adopted them, and they became part of us. This couple has been a real gift to the church. Cory had previously travelled across Canada with a national ministry evangelizing the youth, and he became our youth pastor. He's also a powerful preacher and a gifted leader in the church. There's amazing favor on their lives, wherever they turn. Cory is now breaking new ground with marketplace leaders, and Diana heads up the administration and translation departments for Le Chemin and *HODOS*. They're on our Vision and Direction team, and being among the first leaders to come on board when the apostolic attraction began to operate, they have been faithful companions through the whole process of our transition.

Yvan and Rachel

Rachel and Yvan were serving in a church they loved as young believers. Rachel is a very gifted teacher, passionate for souls, with a remarkable energy and eagerness to minister. In that first church that was heaven on earth for them, the unthinkable happened. A group of people got together to oust the pastor and take over the church, which completely devastated Rachel and Yvan. How was such a thing possible in the house of God? Something in their souls had been broken, and they buried that wound deep inside. They moved to another part of the province, joined a very healthy church, and continued to actively serve the Lord for a number of years. But one day the Lord instructed Yvan to gather their sons, all grown up and living in another area, and move to Gatineau as a family.

They joined our church and became part of our lives. But the deep wound was still there. It took a few years for them to realize they could dream again and trust afresh to call the church home. Today, they are part of our Vision and Direction team, and Rachel teaches all kinds of groups and trains other teachers, both at Le Chemin and elsewhere.

Jean-Pierre and Hélène

When Jean-Pierre and Hélène arrived, they were already seasoned ministers. They had pioneered and pastored a few churches in the province, and Jean-Pierre had ministered internationally for over thirty years. For a number of reasons, they had left the pastoral ministry and had gone back to the marketplace. They explained to me that they were not considering any return to "ministry" in the short-term but wanted to be part of the church life and were willing to help fill the gaps wherever we needed them.

Jean-Pierre is a powerful preacher and really an apostle more than a pastor. He is a strong visionary and always helps me to see farther. I don't know anyone with a clearer revelation on the law of sowing and reaping. To make a long story short, the gifts and experience of this couple were reactivated, and they are now part of our Vision and Direction team, and they lead the international department for *HODOS*, our apostolic network. Jean-Pierre is also one of the founders of a new partnership between the church mountain and the businesses in our city, an organization called *The Ideal Way.*

Reginald and Kareen

I met Reginald at our regional pastors/leaders Christmas supper. We connected immediately. A few weeks after, Reginald and Kareen were sitting in my office. They told Marie and me, "The Lord clearly told us to come with you, but you need to know that after being in ministry for many years in a number of cities and churches, we're done *playing church*. We're looking outside the box, and it's called apostolic."

Reginald and Kareen are both charismatic leaders, strong influencers, gifted beyond measure. In no time, everybody knew them and loved them. Reginald can preach up a storm and leads worship with passion. Kareen is able to mobilize an army of women and launch projects by the dozen. They are on our Vision and Direction team and head up a big chunk of the pastoral department for Le Chemin. This son and daughter totally embraced the apostolic mandate of the house and are pouring their lives into it.

Amy

Amy came as a shy young woman, carrying some hurts from past church experience. It took a while, but we discovered she had an amazing voice and a real prophetic call. We watched the Lord move her step-by-step to the frontlines. She has become one of our worship leaders and a bold prophetess who leads a whole company of prophets in training at Le Chemin.

Tim and Lisa

Tim and Lisa are a gift any church would want to receive. After they ministered in Scotland for a season, things got a bit hard, and they went through a season of wilderness. When they arrived at Le Chemin, we immediately recognized the call they had, and they quickly became involved. Lisa heads up the finances for us, and Tim works with men one-on-one. He has one of the best blogs I have ever seen, so I asked him to write one for this book. Here's Tim:

Restoration
September 16, 2013

The landscape of this nation is littered with people who have lost their way. They have known the hand of God on their lives. They have received His great promises. They have walked with Him in green pastures. They have defeated Goliaths. Yet they have become disillusioned. By sin, by church abuse, or simply by unfulfilled hope, they have had their flames reduced to a flicker. People who once were a danger to the kingdom of darkness are now notches on Satan's belt. I'm sure you can think of a few of these people. Our generation is full of them. The disillusioned have heard the answers. They know the Scriptures. They have heard all the Christian clichés. None of it seems to help, and they are in desperate need of a lifeline. I should know. I spent years in the desert of lost hope. I have tasted the bitterness of the slow fade.

My wife Lisa and I had returned from Scotland in March of 2003 after living and ministering there for three years. Our time in Scotland did not end as we expected, and we returned to Canada to take some time to recover and see where God would direct us. We did not expect He would lead us into a wilderness. I ended up working on the oil rigs in the north, and months became years. With the passing of time came the passing of a sense of purpose. With the passing of purpose came the passing of hope, to the point that I became convinced God was finished with me. I had lost all hope for the future. The passion within me to be used of God to impact my world had been reduced from a bonfire to a flicker. Isaiah 40:27 says, "Why do you say O Jacob... 'My way is hidden from the Lord; my cause is disregarded by my God'?" I felt exactly like Jacob. God was finished with me. Of course I "knew better" (I knew all the Scriptures and all the Christian answers), but none of it seemed to make a difference. Everything inside me felt dead. I figured I had had my shot. It was good while it lasted, but now I was done. There were times when, working on the rigs, I would put down my tools, stare into the heavens, and weep. I longed so much for more, but I had no clue how to reach such a place or even know what it looked like. The heavens seemed closed to me. I was finished. I "lived" like that for a long time.

A couple things helped me get back on the road to hope. One of the greatest factors was the tenacity of a handful of people who refused to give up on me. One of the most persistent was my friend and brother-in-law, Cory, who would call me up from time to time and breathe a little life into my "flicker." Thanks to the investment of a few individuals like Cory, I began to think maybe my life could be redeemed.

During the several visits we had made to visit Cory and Diana (Lisa's sister) in Quebec, we went along with them to their church called Le Chemin. Within this Christian community we found a group of people from the leadership down who were deeply in love with the Lord and passionately committed to serving Him and one another. The love and nurturing I felt deeply impacted me and drew out a longing in my spirit to be restored to the man of faith and passion I once was. As I spoke with their pastor—a remarkable man named Alain Caron—I was amazed. Not only was he full of empathy, insight, and encouragement, but it was clear he was interested in seeing me restored simply for my sake and for the sake of the kingdom. He had nothing to gain personally from investing in me. He simply cared. His desire was purely that I would find fulfillment as I take my place in the kingdom and produce the fruit I was made to produce. What a breath of fresh air! How could I not be drawn in?

In the summer of 2008, my wife Lisa and I packed up our belongings and drove 3,900 kilometers across the country to Quebec. Moving a 42-hour drive from our home in Calgary to a French culture with only one solid family connection, we might as well have been moving to the other side of the planet! When we made the decision to move, we did not have a place to live or a source of income. But we knew we were coming home.

The past five years at Le Chemin have been momentous. There have been difficulties, and there have been miracles. Through it all, my life has been restored, and then some. The call of the Lord on my life is to redeem the disillusioned, and I have found in this place a base of operations from which I can fulfill my destiny with support, security, and freedom.[1]

OUR ALIGNMENT AS A TRIBE

As I wrote in the preface, I met Peter Wagner in June 2012 for our first apostolic conference at Le Chemin. Months before, Doug Schneider had told me about his new alignment with Peter. I must say I was a bit puzzled by the whole thing, but suddenly the Lord spoke clearly to my heart and said, "Invite Peter Wagner, and do it without losing any time." What I felt was that this man had something to deposit in the life of our apostolic center, and for some reason the Lord knew it needed to happen sooner rather than

---

1 You can follow Tim Knapp's blog at www.desertofziph.ca.

later. However, I had no intention at all of entering into further relationship with him after that. I was only looking for a godly deposit.

The conference started on a Thursday night, and Peter stole our hearts right away. We just loved his childlike face, his father's heart, and his godly apostolic authority. Saturday morning, very early, the Lord spoke to me again and said, "I want you to align yourself with Peter." Our first meeting that day was for leaders, and I went ahead with a plan.

After a time of worship, instead of calling Peter to speak, I told him I had something special to do. I first called my wife to join me in the front, as well as our youngest son, David, who also represented his older brother who was not there. Then I called our spiritual dad and mom, Pastors Jean-Claude and Valerie, then all the members of the apostolic team, plus a pastoral couple from another church whom we consider our son and daughter. There must have been about thirty of us standing before Peter, while the rest of the audience kept watching, wondering what I had in mind.

I told Peter I had come before him with my spiritual family to ask for the privilege and honor of aligning with him, not only for myself but as a tribe. I felt like a family of Israel standing before a patriarch! Peter graciously accepted and told us with a smile that this was the first time anyone had asked him to align in such a way.

I can't emphasize enough the value of being properly aligned. This is a principle that has always been in the Scriptures and that we are rediscovering today in the apostolic movement. Let the bones come together to receive the breath of life—a more abundant life!

CHAPTER 6

Activating the Saints to Exponential Life

THE BEST PORTION

One of the main characteristics of an apostolic center is the emphasis it has on equipping people for ministry. I call this *activating the saints to exponential life*. Why do I say that? Jesus said, "My food is to do the will of him who sent me and to finish his work" (John 4:34). If fulfilling the apostolic mandate was what gave Jesus His sustenance, the same should be true of us, and we should find a quality of life in our activation that is incomparable to anything else. I believe this is what Jesus had in mind when He said, "I have come that they may have life, and have it to the full" (John 10:10). That abundant life is not just reserved for our future state, but it also has a lot to do with our active involvement right now. Our food is to do the will of Him who sent us!

So when we call people to be active members in the body of Christ, we are actually offering them the best part. Where else would they find the sweetest communion with the Holy Spirit if not in the fields of His harvest? We often have misperceptions about intimacy. After many ups and downs in their courtship, the Shulamite finally told her beloved where their union would be consummated: "Let us go early to the vineyards to see if the vines have budded, if their blossoms have opened, and if the pomegranates are in bloom— there I will give you my love" (Song of Sol. 7:12). She was right, as the early disciples also found out. The place of fellowship with the Lord is still in the context of our ongoing mission: "Then the disciples went out and preached everywhere, and *the Lord worked with them* and confirmed his word by the signs that accompanied it" (Mark 16:20, emphasis added).

TRAIN AND SEND

With this in mind, we view our apostolic center as a training camp and a sending base. Our approach is hands-on rather than just theory. Following the model Jesus developed when He sent the twelve, then the seventy, we look for opportunities to let the saints do the ministry rather than doing it for them.

Even the Sunday morning service can become a training session. At times we have prayed like this, "Holy Spirit, we're asking You this morning to do a workshop with all of us and activate the gift of prophecy." Then we have people form small groups and practice on one another. At other times, we have asked for gifts of knowledge for healings to be manifested. We then gave a chance to all who felt they had received something to say it, and then those who identified with the condition stood as people around prayed for them. We witnessed many healings that way, and it was not "from the pulpit" or "at the altar" (although we also do those things at other times). What a joy it is when the whole sanctuary turns into a bubbling boot camp filled with ordinary people becoming extraordinary saints!

The message we consistently teach is that every single saint, without exception, has a divine calling and capacity to impact the world with supernatural ability. We relentlessly repeat that, through the blood of Jesus Christ and in the power of the Holy Spirit, we have been made agents of the kingdom of God, carriers of the glory, living gates of heaven on earth, conquerors, and world changers.

We reject passive Christianity and consider ourselves to be releasers of the life He has poured into us.

THRIVING

What happened over time is that our church culture changed to one that contains a dynamic eagerness to see things happen and an expectation that the Holy Spirit will move. There is a *buzz* around the apostolic center.

In a French culture, which is considered hard and resistant to the gospel, we are finally seeing steady growth with the regular addition of newly saved people. Baptisms are done a few times a year, with explosions of joy every time. People are bringing friends, who bring other friends. Young families are filling the place, and we are experiencing a real baby boom! A solid third of the congregation is under twelve, and new ones keep being announced. It seems the natural and the spiritual are in sync over this. Healthy reproduction is a good sign; love is in the air.

That also works for ministries and cell groups. We use the "Free Market Cells" model, with a cycle of two semesters per year, and we now have to add a third shorter session to replace the summer break because some people just don't want to stop! Isn't that cool? The number of cells keeps increasing every semester. That is what happens when people really get the apostolic vision. They are activated, and they all want to do something. They come with projects and ideas, proposals and initiatives. The new challenge for the administration team is no longer to mobilize people but instead to juggle schedules and room usage, trying to coordinate and accommodate the flow of activity that's constantly released. We used to explain that the word *cell* did not refer to prison cells but to the cells in a beehive. Well, the beehive has sure become a reality at our address!

It came to a point where I had to address the situation because, according to normal reasoning, it seemed we had too many cells for a congregation of our size. I presented it this way on a Sunday morning: "There are so many cell groups ready to be launched that it doesn't make sense. But when I thought about it, I felt the Lord was asking me why I wanted to put a limit on it. If there are two hundred people in the congregation, why couldn't we have two hundred cells? Or even more? Everyone here could lead a cell and reach out. We need to shift our focus from our church to the city." That's apostolic! That day we made one more step toward a kingdom mindset. We haven't come close to having the number of cells match the number of seats used on Sunday mornings (this would now be around three hundred), but we keep growing, and the vision is there in front of us.

ALL NATIONS

From time to time, I look at the people and tell them, "You are the best church in the whole world." Technically, one could argue with that statement, but my heart is totally irrational in that matter. I sometimes see a brilliance coming in the room and everybody glowing with supernatural beauty. The church is really the reflection of Christ. He said, "My house will be called a house of prayer for all nations" (Mark 11:17). This is what I see developing before my eyes from week to week.

We are a spiritual house made up of many nations and languages. Our first vision is for the French Canadians, then the French nations of the world. But we also have a heart for the nation of Canada and for all the nations of the world, with a special love and commitment toward Israel as the first of all nations in God's heart.

So that you can better understand the DNA of Le Chemin, let me paint a very broad picture of Canada for you. The country is made up of four people groups: the First Peoples (First Nations, Inuit, and Metis), the French Canadians (originally from France), the English Canadians (originally from England, Ireland, and Scotland), and the later immigrants from all over the world. There is a long trail of tension among the first three groups and many sins in our history. That is why you rarely see them fellowshipping under the same roof for very long. But we know redemption is coming to heal this land, and we will be one people united in God's love. Le Chemin is part of that redemption.

It started with Pastor Jean-Claude marrying Valerie, an English girl from New Brunswick. They were a prophetic picture of the unity the Lord wanted to see in His body. From the beginning of the church, they held bilingual meetings. More than thirty-five years later, we are still functioning in that same setting, and our congregation is made up of French and English living in harmony together. We sing in both languages, preach with an interpreter, and laugh and cry in the tongue of our choice. We have covenantal friendship with First Nations leaders Chief Kenny and Louise Blacksmith, true apostles of forgiveness and reconciliation in Canada, and an ongoing commitment to Jewish friends in Israel.

But to complete this picture, we need to mention that we have around twenty nations represented in the house. When the law of apostolic attraction kicked into gear, they started to come. We embraced everyone in their diversity, and we became one. This is absolutely true. We don't have any cultural cells or special nights for special groups. We are all together and refuse to be separated by our national differences. We celebrate each other in the gifts we represent and eat good food we never knew existed!

I made that long parenthesis so you can understand that, in our context, when I talk about activating the saints to exponential life, it launches in all directions and has the potential to touch the diverse cultures and spheres of society. We are called to be the picture of the house of the Father on the earth, with one long table for all. When we walk in that kind of unity, there's authority to speak and bring the influence of the kingdom of God in the affairs of the world.

In the next pages, I'm going to tell you a few stories of what can happen when saints are activated.

A ROOF FOR HAITI

The Reluctant Prophet

In November 2009, I visited the United Evangelical Church, a small independent church in Port-au-Prince, Haiti. We were meeting in the basement of a building that had no roof. The construction had been stopped years before due to lack of funds. The congregation was made up of the poorest people I had ever met, right in the center of a desolate slum. Lloyd, the new pastor, was a true son of the community, raised in that church. When I got up to preach, I looked at him, then at the founding pastor, now a frail old man, honored and loved by all, who was sitting at the back of the church, and the spirit of prophecy suddenly rose in me.

"Your church will become an agent of change in this community. You will affect the economy of the whole neighborhood and bring transformation and prosperity to it. You will be a sign to the community that a slum can be transformed. And the Lord says that the signal for you will be when a roof is placed on top of the building."

I couldn't believe what was coming out of my mouth. At the same time that I was boldly declaring these words, knowing the gift of prophecy was in operation, my thoughts were racing anxiously in my head, and I was telling myself, "Why am I setting up these good people for disappointment? Where in the world will the money come from for this roof? There's no way you can raise what it takes right now, and they have even less chance of raising any money at all themselves."

But the words kept coming out with force. Pointing to the old retired pastor at the back, I continued, "And you pastor, you will see this happen with your own eyes."

The Earthquake

A few weeks after I was back in Canada, the destructive earthquake hit Haiti, on January 12, 2010, killing 150,000 people. Pastor Lloyd was in the middle of his tiny house when the shaking started.

He just had time to grab his youngest daughter and cover her with his own body before the cement roof fell on them. They were miraculously saved, although he was hurt and needed surgery on one of his feet. But many families in the church lost loved ones—dads and moms, sons and daughters.

Their school building completely collapsed, but the church itself remained standing, with cracks and damages that could be repaired. I went to visit them a few times after the earthquake, ministering and encouraging them with the teams I brought with me, but I still wondered about that roof.

A Spark of Faith

At the end of April 2011, I took another trip to Haiti. As I was witnessing the resilience of my Haitian brothers once again—their faith, their perseverance, and the love they had for one another—suddenly something happened in me, and faith was created almost two years after I had given the prophecy. I turned to Marculey, the son of the founding pastor, and in a surge of enthusiasm I told him, "Let's meet with an engineer and find out what it takes to reinforce the foundations of the church and put a roof on it!"

The total cost was estimated to $25,000 Canadian, and it was decided that we would give the contract to Haitian professionals rather than trying to bring in Canadian laborers. I told them to start making the plans and that our church in Canada would come up with the money—but I had no idea how!

Vision Breeds Faith

I came back home with that project burning in my heart, and I preached a message titled "A Roof for Haiti." That was Sunday morning, May 8, 2011. Remember, we were in the second year of transition, the year of the shift from a traditional local church to an apostolic center. I told the people that the end-times apostolic church is one that takes care of the people of God, and we needed to stir ourselves to good works and raise $25,000 to put a roof over the church we supported in Port-au-Prince that had so badly suffered from the earthquake.

During the week, Jean-Pierre, one of our main leaders, asked to see me. We met in a restaurant, and he told me he had on his heart to spearhead the fundraising efforts for the project. I confirmed to him he was actually the person I had in mind for this.

Leaning back, he started to explain his plan. "I'm looking at a period of one year to complete that project and…"

I stopped him right away, looked directly into his eyes, and said, "What about before the end of this year?"

He looked back at me to see if I was joking. We were a congregation of about 150 people, counting children, with no money in the bank and nobody among us with big bucks. But Jean-Pierre is a man of faith who loves challenges.

When he realized I was dead serious, he locked his faith with mine and said, "Okay, we'll do it." At that moment, I knew it was a done deal.

Mega Yard Sale

Yvan suggested we do a mega yard sale on the church grounds. On July 23, we had not only a full yard with more than twenty tables of articles that people had donated for us to sell, but our youth also operated a car wash in front of the building, and inside we had a hair dressing salon, a manicure table, a jewelry shop, and a free prayer booth. That was a fantastic day with a huge participation from the congregation. By the time we finished, we had collected more than $8,000.

A Historic Offering

Jean-Pierre announced that we would prepare for a revival offering on Thanksgiving Sunday, October 9. The instructions were to seek the Lord over the next number of weeks about the amount we needed to sow; that would be the only offering we would take for our project. We reminded everyone of the plan from Sunday to

Sunday, with a goal of $17,000, since with the monies received from the yard sale we had already raised $8,000. I'm not sure anyone believed we could actually reach $17,000 in a single offering, but we hoped to get as close to that as possible.

Thanksgiving Sunday came, and we devoted the service to the revival offering. After a passionate exhortation from Jean-Pierre, we started to bring our offerings in an electric atmosphere, shouting and dancing, the worship team playing strong. We placed two baskets in the front and also had a debit machine for electronic giving in another room. People started to put loads of envelopes, checks, and cash in the baskets and lined up to give using the debit machine. We had a team of people counting in the office at the back, while we continued to sing and worship, waiting for the results.

The count for the first basket came in—over $10,000! The people started to roar. We sang and rejoiced some more, and then the count for the second basket came in—*another* $16,000! Then the count for the electronic giving was announced—$6,000! We had collected a total of *$32,000!* A historic and miraculous offering had taken place!

Angelic Visitation

After the totaling, Amy released this vision:

> At the beginning of the service, I saw a category of angels who were like scribes who had come to take note of all that would happen this morning.

> Then during the offering, I felt the Lord was pleased to see people give. In fact, I saw the image of the bride clothed in white coming before Jesus with an offering basket. It was glorious. There was an interaction between the two of them. It was so pleasing to the Lord that He declared He would give it back to her in anointing, in honor, in glory, in power. There will be an increase in anointing, in revelation,

119

in order to go to another level in Him.

After that I saw another kind of angels, much taller, who came down to take the place of the others. They looked like warriors. They came with gifts for us. Anointing, supernatural, revelation, healing—all that relates to the ministry of the church.

I feel we have entered a new dimension and that the offering we gave broke many things. Among other things, our hearts were revealed, and it pleased God.

Fundraising Supper

The following Saturday we had a fundraising supper with distinguished guests of honor—the ambassador of Haiti, the mayor and his wife, and a number of representatives from the business community. We showed a video of our project, had a few speeches from the dignitaries, received a check from one of the corporations represented, took an offering—and by the end of the evening, we knew that for the entire project we had now reached $50,000— double our original objective.

Accelerated Developments

With the $50,000, not only was a roof built, but the whole building was renovated, and brand new pews replaced the flimsy benches they had before. On February 19, 2012, in Port-au-Prince, eight members of Le Chemin attended the inauguration.

That church, and I must also say the leadership of Pastor Lloyd, took an accelerated curve of growth from that development. The attendance has already doubled to four hundred people, and Lloyd has told me they are making plans to build a balcony. They are truly sending a signal of hope to the entire community and are becoming the reference point for rising out of the cycle of poverty. Let me explain.

In all our exchanges, we always followed a philosophy of empowering our friends in Haiti. We insisted in our messages and teachings that it was *their faith* that produced the change they experienced and that even the money we brought was but a result of the activation of that faith expressed in prayer. We made sure to let them direct the whole project, and they did wonders, far more than could normally be expected for the amount of money available. Through all this, they truly rose up as a people and started to dream again and to take ownership of their success. This, more than the finances, is the victory that flies high above their roof.

One of the challenges their neighborhood has been facing for a long time is the deterioration of their streets. The situation has gotten so bad that cars can't even use the road unless they have four-wheel drive. That is why I was so happy when I received a phone call telling me the mayor had summoned the population of the district to make the official announcement that the street passing right in front of the church would be completely redone. And where did the mayor announce this good news to the people? At the church!

The last time I went to Haiti, I noticed the young boys of the church going around and asking people if they could shine their shoes. I had never seen them do that before, and I wondered why they were doing so now. Then in the service, through my broken Creole, I picked up they were talking about a special offering and some activities the youth were doing, but I wasn't sure what it was all about. I leaned toward one of the men and asked for an explanation. "Oh, he's talking about a special offering we are preparing and the activities the kids are doing to raise funds for our project. We want to put a roof over a poor church in Jacmel." I could have wept.

One of the characteristics of an apostolic center should be that they enable other churches to reach their apostolic destiny. This is what's happening with our friends. Lloyd is now giving leadership to an increasing number of churches in different cities and other parts of the country. He is developing as a trusted and loving apostle and his church as a flourishing apostolic center.

More to Come

As we continued to partner with our friends in Haiti, two other Canadian churches joined with us for a long-term plan to empower the community. We are making plans to rebuild the school that collapsed in the earthquake (at the moment they hold their classes in the basement of the church). We call this project: *A School for Haiti*. Then we have started to build a ten-kilometer road in the mountains to connect an isolated population to health care and education. This project is *A Road for Haiti*. The only way to get to those mountains at the moment is through hours of trekking, with people carrying merchandise on their heads and using mules and donkeys. We were there in 2012, and a nurse we brought with us helped deliver a baby who otherwise would have died, and most probably the mother would have as well. You see, the apostolic ministry is not about theology and speech alone; it's about taking the gospel of the kingdom and applying it to a fractured world in need of transformation.[1]

THE IDEAL WAY

The Vision of a Young Entrepreneur

I must confess something. After we took our miracle offering of $32,000, I was scared the revenues of the church would go down for a while until people recovered from their big gift (I know, I know, not very glorious for an apostle, but I'm trying to be transparent). In fact, it turned out to be the opposite. Giving went up a notch from that day and never came down after.

However, I didn't yet know that would be the case when, just a few weeks after that offering, Nicholas, a young entrepreneur from our church, said to me, "We don't have a program for Christmas baskets. I'd like to do something to bless our community. Would

---

1   If you'd like to help us in our effort in Haiti, visit our website at: http://www.lechemin.ca/mission_comp-e.php.

you be interested in moving in that direction? I would do the fundraising among the business community in the city, and the church would pack the boxes and do the delivery."

Nicholas and his wife, Nancy, had joined Le Chemin about a year before. Prior to that, they had been part of a very conservative church. Discovering the charismatic lifestyle in our midst had given them a surge of joy and activated them for a whole new vision of Christianity, where Nicholas felt he could finally apply his entrepreneurial drive to furthering the kingdom of God.

Three Weeks to Deliver

Time was short; we were already at the end of October, and I knew people needed to rest after all the activities we had just finished for Haiti. For those reasons, I was not sure it was the right timing to launch another project. But Nicholas is a very enthusiastic young man, and somehow I just couldn't say no to him. After all, when you keep activating people into an apostolic mindset, you have to be ready to see them rise up with visions.

I asked him how much money he thought he could raise. He said he had a goal of $25,000. "Okay; give it a try," I told him. I needed someone from the newly-formed Vision and Direction team to walk with him in this, so I asked Jean-Pierre. He said yes right away.

Nicholas went to work, and in three weeks he had not only reached his goal but gone substantially beyond it, gathering $37,500 from fifteen entrepreneurs in the city. Jean-Pierre put a large team together and built a plan to find out where and how the baskets should be distributed.

The strategy was two-fold: Make a list of families in need through the church contacts, and work with existing charitable organizations like Big Brothers Big Sisters, Single Parents Association, Option Women at Work, and others.

The day of packing and distribution was a real party. We packed the boxes in the sanctuary of the church, turned it upside down, got the carpet dirty and had a blast! Baskets with a value of $250 were distributed to 150 families.

Explosive Progression

Shortly after New Year's, we organized a formal gala supper to thank everyone involved in the project. We had all the volunteers, the business people, and the mayor in attendance. People wept when we showed the video of all that had been done. Then Nicholas launched the vision for 2012: a target of $100,000!

What do you think? Did Nicholas reach that second-year goal? He sure did! Forty-one entrepreneurs joined in, and baskets with a value of $550 were distributed to 300 families, for a total of $165,000; we had $45,000 leftover, which we wanted to invest in specific needs during the year.

A New Partnership in the City

Seeing that progression, we developed the vision further and established a new organization. The two main players had been Le Chemin and the company Nicholas is closely associated with, called Ideal Protein. Since Le Chemin means The Way, Jean-Pierre came up with the idea of combining the two names and calling the new organization The Ideal Way, an explosive partnership between leaders from two spheres of influence in the city, church and business.

The Ideal Way's goal now is to devote one-third of the funds received to Christmas baskets and the remaining two-thirds to bringing transformation to the lives of specific families—single-parent families and families where children face poverty challenges. We want to help them pass to the next level and have no more need of Christmas baskets in the future. Examples of that range from paying the tuition for parents to go back to school, to paying daycare fees to make it possible for parents to have activities outside the home, to buying a car for a single parent to open up possibilities for better work, to paying for professional help or support.

Attacking poverty at its roots should certainly be an objective that apostolic centers pursue in their cities and nations. Activating the saints to exponential life is releasing the creativity and power needed to do it.

A SINGLE MOM TOUCHES THE CITY

Anik is a single mother with four children. They live in a neighborhood where the city manages low-rent units for people who cannot afford high market rents. Because she was alone to raise her kids, Anik has not been able to work outside the home for many years.

When we started to activate people to come up with cell group ideas, Anik decided she wanted to try something. With the encouragement she received in the church, she had already started to develop a strong artistic gift, which had been dormant, for painting and creating art objects. Her idea was to use this gift to implement a cell group right where she lived, in the community center just beside her apartment.

She met with the administrators of the community center and proposed a workshop on personal development through arts. They liked the idea but were hesitant about the spiritual aspect of it, as they had people from different religions in the neighborhood. Anik responded that she had no intention of forcing her faith on anyone and wanted to let everybody find his or her own expression through art. The only thing she insisted on doing was to pray at the beginning and at the end, and if this was offensive to anyone, they could walk away for that short moment and come back without any problem.

There was a long period of waiting before they gave their answer. They had never opened the door to a Christian activity in their center, and they were obviously very cautious about it. They finally said yes and even provided snacks and juices for Anik to give to the participants.

It became a huge success! Exploring themes like self-worth,

respect, love, and peace, people from that neighborhood found a way to express their hearts in amazing artistic creations. At the end of the semester, an exposition was organized in the center, and it was stunning to see that without any direct instructions from Anik regarding faith, Christian symbolism was highly present throughout the works.

Summer passed; then another semester started. The community center was pleased to again open its doors to Anik. In November, a gala dinner was organized by the city for all the volunteers in the city. Our city has a population of 270,000 people, so there are many volunteers.

Anik was happy to be there, watching all the people who had given so much of their time to bless their community. When the organizers mentioned an award would be given for the volunteer of the year, she looked at some of the elderly people who, in her eyes, were "professional volunteers" and waited to see which one would receive the prize, rejoicing ahead of time for them. When they started by saying that the award this year was going to a single mother, her heart stopped. She couldn't believe it. She had never even given a single thought to that possibility. But it was true. Anik had been chosen as the volunteer of the year for 2012.

I like that story. It illustrates the redemptive power of the apostolic activation. Anik has continued, and she has been approached with the possibility of establishing her workshop in other community centers in the city. Discussions have taken place to offer her a course in community animation and to give her a paid position with the community centers.

WHEN THE SAINTS GO MARCHING IN

I could tell many more stories of the abundant life that is released when people are activated for the kingdom of God. I could speak of Jocelyn (the same you read about in Chapter 1) and *Café Expression* he operates on Saturday nights with artists from all over. I could mention Pauline and Robin reaching out to their village or

Augustin and Aimée, Jeanne, and many more.

We have seen an explosion of ministries taking place in an atmosphere that became contagious. In the next chapter, we'll dive into that contagious atmosphere.

CHAPTER 7

Party at the Gate –
Ladder Included

JACOB'S DREAM

How awesome is this place! This is none other than the house of God; this is the gate of heaven (Gen. 28:17).

I don't think we could find a more brilliant way to describe the dynamics of how our weekly apostolic meetings should be than what Jacob said when he woke up from his dream. His sentence is one of those extraordinary nuggets in the Bible that, in just a few words, succeeds in framing complex and supernatural realities.

Within the human heart lies a deep desire to be part of a house, and if this house is God's house, we know this is good news. An immediate sense of peace and security is released at the mention of it. This is because of the presence of the Father. His is a reassuring presence. He is the heart of the house, and He surrounds Himself with many sons and daughters. Harmony lives among them— times of laughter and action, times of quiet smiles and rest; it is the warmth of a healthy family. Because of the love that fills this house, we can find no safer place to celebrate with our whole hearts.

I don't know if you have ever been part of a house party, where you pull out the guitars and people start clapping their hands and singing, and you move the table and chairs against the walls to make more room to dance in the kitchen, and the kids get so excited they start jumping and running, and more people show up at the door wanting to join in. Jacob said, "This is none other than the house of God." Our Sunday mornings at Le Chemin sometimes feel like that.

However, this picture wouldn't be complete without the revelation Jacob received about the invisible side of things: "This is the gate of heaven." Why did he say that? He had just seen a ladder in his dream that was resting on the earth, with its top reaching to heaven. Angels were ascending and descending on it, while the Lord God Himself stood above it and declared mighty promises for Jacob's life and for his descendants. Jacob realized he was standing at the threshold of a reality that superseded the natural world. He understood that God's house is a portal to God's domain.

We make a huge mistake when we separate those two parts in our church life. What most traditional churches offer to people is a social fabric. Everything is about community and catering to the needs of people and their families—without an interwoven supernatural element, unless you categorize brotherly love as supernatural.

Christianity without the supernatural dimension is often reduced to trying to make people become nicer and nicer by having them listen to good messages; that is not exactly the radical shift Jesus suffered death for.

On the other hand, we all know churches or people who always live on Jacob's ladder, never touching the ground! We need to remind ourselves that the ladder is resting on the earth.

So, should we favor the *house* part or the *ladder* part? Both. Apostolic centers actually pull from the two ends of Jacob's revelation and happily live in the tension of their union. We offer a healthy environment where people can have genuine relationships under the supernatural cloud of glory that has come to rest on the earth.

The manifestation of this cloud of glory is what separates us from any other social group, regardless of how noble those might be. Moses understood that clearly when he said to the Lord, "If your Presence does not go with us, do not send us up from here… What else will distinguish me and your people from all the other people on the face of the earth?" (Exod. 33:15–16).

The supernatural presence of God is definitely the strongest catalyst to thrust people into redemptive encounters that change their lives forever. Let me give you a snapshot of one of our Sunday mornings to illustrate what I mean. This one is a fictional reconstruction from various personal comments and stories we have received rather than an exact report from one meeting in particular, but it gives a faithful picture of the dynamics we are used to.

THE SUNDAY EXPERIENCE

Surely the Lord is in this place, and I was not aware of it (Gen. 28:16).

10:20

Monique had never gone to a church other than Catholic, and even there, the only times she would go were for weddings and funerals and maybe once in a while at Christmas and Easter. When she was a teen, like most of her friends, she had stopped giving any attention to religion. She was now forty-two, divorced, with shared custody of two boys, had a steady job, and wondered if she was on the edge of a burnout.

As she turned into the driveway of the church, she suddenly felt a light trembling inside her. What was happening? She was not anxious or worried, Martine and Robert had invited her many times, and she would meet them inside; maybe she was a bit nervous, but why that trembling? Was it just an impression? She looked at her hands, and they seemed steady on the steering wheel.

Michael, one of the parking attendants, gave her a big smile and pointed to one of the few spots left. It would be a packed Sunday. She parked her car, took the keys out of the ignition, and when she tried to open her purse to put them in, she realized her hands were definitely trembling. And she felt a big urge to cry. But why?

A minivan pulled right beside her. This was a family of five: Eli, Nathalie, and their three young kids. They had come a few months ago, just arriving in the city, having spent the previous year in Montreal. They were from the Congo-Kinshasa, and Eli was finishing his masters in International Development. The kids started to run toward the entrance, where Marc, a young boy their age, was waving at them with both arms.

Eli and Nathalie had been active members of a large church in Kinshasa; then in Montreal they had tried a church mainly attended by Africans, then another one that was mostly white. When they moved to Gatineau, Congolese friends told them about Le Chemin.

Nathalie said hello to Monique and started to walk with her while Eli quickly went ahead, shouting to the kids, "Don't run!" But they were already inside.

10:25

Greeters welcomed them at the door, and Monique immediately found Martine and Robert, who were waiting for her in the foyer. They hugged and told her how excited they were to see her. Monique just hoped her trembling didn't show, but there was so much movement in that foyer that nobody would notice. People were talking loudly, joking, and laughing, walking all around, with kids running in between—lots of kids.

This was very different from what Monique remembered from her last visit to a church. In fact, so different that it didn't even feel like a church, at least, not according to what she had seen so far.

Eli and Nathalie had also been surprised the first time they came. They were use to charismatic churches, but this one was definitely the most friendly and active one they had ever seen. Eli had come wearing a suit and tie but quickly realized he was almost the only one dressed like that. Even the pastor was wearing jeans and a dress shirt. Eli had *never* seen that in any church he attended. However, as the weeks went by, Eli got used to that style and adopted it as his own.

10:30

They went through another team of greeters and entered the auditorium. There must have been close to two hundred people in there. Monique's first impression was that, besides the size, there was no big difference between this room and the foyer. The aisles were filled with people standing and talking; others were sitting and chatting with the people in the rows in front of or behind them; others were walking around; kids were everywhere; and about fifteen people on the stage seemed to be having lots of fun in the midst of all kinds of instruments and microphone stands.

Martine and Robert introduced Monique to a bunch of people, many more than she could retain in terms of new names. She noticed there were just about as many black people as white, that she was hearing French conversations weaved through English ones, that it was noisy, that it looked kind of chaotic—but overall that it felt very joyful. No, it was not disorder. It was something else that she was trying to put her finger on—freedom? Yes, that's the impression she was getting inside of her. But why in the world was she feeling like she had to hold back her tears?

10:35

A man started to speak from the front, and his voice, through the sound system, projected throughout the auditorium. "This is Alain, our pastor," Martine told Monique.

"Hi everybody," he said. "Welcome to Le Chemin. This is our apostolic center, a church that believes in people being activated to change the world. You have come to the right place today to receive new life and be empowered. The Lord Jesus Christ is the King we serve. Come on, please stand and give Him glory!"

People stood and started to clap their hands loudly. Some shouted and a few even whistled. There was still a flow of people coming in, and a lot of movement around the auditorium. Monique saw Nathalie and Eli, who had found a place a few rows in front of her, hugging other people who were arriving, as their kids ran to the front, where a number of other children were also going. A few little girls went around Marie, Alain's wife, who bent forward to talk to them, smiling.

The music suddenly exploded, loud and clear, in a French song that the crowd seemed to know well, a mix of rock and gospel, fast and happy. A number of people joined the kids in the front, mainly women, and picked up flags of different colors to dance with to the music's rhythm. A few kids also took smaller flags, while other children just stood there, with adults watching them in case they forgot why they were at the front and started to run around and play.

Monique had never seen anything like it! There were even guys with professional cameras moving around as the whole thing was streamed live on the Internet. She looked at Martine and saw she had her eyes closed, both hands raised, singing.

10:50

The band played songs both in French and English, alternating between the two languages without any fixed pattern, and sometimes even launched into lyrics that were not on the screen, improvising. Monique was wondering how they did that, but also couldn't help but realize they were playing and singing with such passionate abandonment that they were operating under inspiration. She heard some people not far from her sing in tongues, which was quite different, but Martine had already told her about that before she came.

People were still coming in, even though they were late, and it didn't seem to bother anyone. There were now around three hundred people in the place, and the atmosphere was electric.

11:00

Monique saw a young woman leave her seat and go whisper something in Alain's ear. He nodded and gave her the microphone. She went on the stage, the band lowered the volume of the music, and she started to pray in French in a passionate way:

Holy Spirit we welcome You. Come and do Your work. Change us. Baptize us afresh. Pour Your fire on us. Come and search our hearts. Bring a separation between what is natural and what is spiritual. Give us boldness for You. We say yes to this new season that You are bringing, and we embrace it.

Another lady immediately came beside her to interpret what she said into English. Various people had their hands lifted toward heaven; some were just standing with their eyes closed. The band kept playing in the background. The woman continued:

And I feel the Lord is saying that we are called to arise in our gifts and in our callings. We must take our stand! It is a time to define our position in Him. It is a time to enter into the supernatural, for our faith to rise, to see miracles, and as a result show who God is.

At that moment, another woman came on the stage and was given the microphone:

God will be with us wherever we go, and He will confirm the word we preach. If we preach deliverance, we will see people delivered; if we preach salvation, we will see people saved; and if we preach healing, we will see people healed. Open your mouths everywhere you go, because God says, "I will always be with you."

People cheered, and the band got louder. Alain came on the stage and said, "We don't have to wait to enter into what the Lord just spoke to us prophetically. I feel one of the gifts He's activating today is the word of knowledge for healings. Did anyone receive one while we were worshipping?"

Eli and Nathalie both raised their hands, as well as five or six other people in the auditorium. Alain pointed to Eli first, who said, "I saw a picture of a man with a torn ligament in the right knee." Alain looked at the crowd and asked, "Is there a man here with this condition?" A man at the back raised his hand. Alain told him, "Okay, just stay there for now; we'll pray for you in a moment." Then he pointed to Nathalie. She said she had felt a sharp pain in her stomach. Two persons stood up, identifying with that pain. And it went on like that for the few others who said they had a word of knowledge.

Then Alain asked the people around those who had stood up to lay hands on them and pray in the name of Jesus. Huddles were formed everywhere in the room. After a few minutes, he asked the people receiving prayer to check if they were healed or if there was any change. Right away three or four raised their hands, and people started to shout for joy. He instructed the people to pray a second time for those who were not healed yet. A couple more received a healing.

11:15

Monique was now sobbing uncontrollably, watching all this supernatural activity around her, and she was not the only one to be moved like that. Alain told the people that what they were witnessing was the goodness of the Lord.

He asked how many people were visiting Le Chemin for the first time. About a dozen hands came up. The rest of the congregation clapped to welcome them, and ushers quickly made their way to them to give them a welcome package.

Then Alain explained that what people were feeling was actually the presence of God, that Jesus was alive and well, and that He desired to have a personal relationship with them. He then addressed the whole crowd and said that if there was anyone there who didn't have a personal relationship with Jesus, there was no reason why they should leave without knowing Him, if they wanted to do so.

He then invited the people to bring up their offerings and dismissed the children to their classes. People moved around for a while, greeting one another, chatting, and visiting.

11:25

Alain called the people back to their seats and made a few announcements. He mentioned that there were many cell groups that met during the week and also invited everyone to a special time of prayer at 5:30 a.m. on Monday morning. Eli stood up and shouted "Hallelujah!" People started to laugh. He also announced that there would be a youth night on Friday and *Café Expression* on Saturday night, which would feature a band from Toronto.

Alain then greeted three Members of Parliament present that Sunday and a First Nations chief and his wife seated in the balcony.

A young entrepreneur came up to give an update on a project to provide teenagers from single parent families with tools to become socially responsible, which was done in partnership with business people in the city. He wanted to approach the mayor with the idea and asked the congregation to stand and pray with him for that to happen.

11:35

Alain then said, "Okay, let's get ready to look into God's Word together. I want to tell you there's no way around this one: If you want to grow in your Christian life, you need to spend time in the Bible. I will not be the one preaching this morning; Pastor Reginald is the one who will share with us. But before he comes, let me just mention this: We have gathered here today to celebrate the Lord and to be equipped for what's ahead. We are ambassadors for the kingdom of God. We are sent to bring the influence of Jesus in every sphere of society where God has placed us. That's our apostolic mandate as a people. We are carriers of the glory of God shattering the darkness of this world to set the captives free. We are an army of compassion and humility, walking with authority. We proclaim the kingship of Jesus everywhere we go. We tell people they have to turn away from their sins and embrace Jesus to receive eternal life. We are world changers and the devil's nightmare." People cheered.

He continued, "My role as the apostolic leader here is to submit to the Holy Spirit and be a facilitator for what He wants to do. My goal is to see all of you released in your divine calling. The healings we have seen this morning are a practice for what we ought to do all week outside these walls. Even creation is groaning to see Christ revealed in you. The blood of Jesus has opened the way for all of us. Let's keep pressing in. The kingdom of heaven is at hand!" That gave way to another round of applause. "Now, please welcome Pastor Reginald."

11:40

Monique had stopped crying and was feeling like she had entered a different world. Pastor Reginald talked about the gifts of the Holy Spirit and how they can be used in our daily lives. He explained how Joseph and the prophet Daniel, each in their days, influenced whole nations because God gave them a supernatural ability to interpret dreams. He showed with passages of the Bible that when we are born again, we gain access to God's throne of grace and to the gifts He has for us.

12:20

At the end of his message, he said, "We want to make sure everyone here has the opportunity to be born again and receive eternal life. This is where everything we talked about must start. If this is new to you, chances are you have not come alone here, but someone invited you. I'm going to ask everyone to turn to the people beside you and ask them if they need to give their lives to Jesus. And if they do, I want you to pray with them, right where you are, and lead them to Christ."

There was movement in the seats, and everywhere in the auditorium people started to talk. Some just kept chatting, while others began to pray with the person next to them.

12:25

Reginald said, "Great, please look up here. How many of you prayed to accept the Lord?" People raised their hands at different places in the room. One of them was Monique, and her face was glowing. Martine and Robert were still beside her, but this time they were the ones weeping, happy for their friend. People cheered.

He continued, "Let's ask the Holy Spirit to activate His gifts in us now. Let's all stand and ask together for a mighty baptism of the Holy Spirit with love and power. I'm going to ask the members of the apostolic team to move around and lay hands on people, and if you have an urgent need for anything, make your way to the front so we can pray with you. But let's now ask the Holy Spirit to empower us with supernatural ability to preach the gospel of the kingdom with authority and with signs and miracles."

12:35

Monique wasn't sure what had happened. She found herself trying to get up from the carpet where she was laying. Some people were on the floor like her. Those standing were praying for each other, some were weeping, some were laughing, and other people just stood there with their eyes closed. The worship team was playing, and the kids were back from their classes. Martine helped Monique to her feet and with a smile said, "Welcome home."

12:45

Monique felt a great peace in her heart. A peace like she had never known. A peace she had no words to describe. It felt like she had rested deeply after years of struggle. The trembling was still there and would stay for a few days, but it was now very light, more like a feeling she had inside her.

People were starting to leave, but many were lingering and visiting. It would be a good hour before the place was empty. Some of the young adults just loved to stay longer and chitchat.

"You want to come and eat with us?" Martine asked Monique.

Monique replied slowly, like someone coming out of the clouds, "Yeah, that would be great. But I don't know if I can drive right now." They both started to laugh.

Behind them, they heard the voice of Eli calling Alain, "Hey, Apostle, come here, I have a big hug for you! So, when will you come over and eat some good African food? My wife is the best cook you know."

Alain replied, "I don't know about that, you haven't tasted *my* wife's food!"

"But that's *Canadian food,*" Eli said.

Alain answered, "I thought you wanted to become Canadian." And they both started to laugh, walking arm in arm toward the entrance.

"You know something?" Monique asked Martine. She paused, as if thinking deeply, then looked directly into her friend's eyes and said, "God is in this place, and I didn't even know it until today."

PART 2

Linking Apostolic Centers into Apostolic Networks

CHAPTER 8

A Power Grid for
Territorial Governance

NETWORKS

I've already mentioned that Paul linked the new communities of believers he established into networks and that apostolic centers occupied a central and strategic place in that structure. But what is a network?

The term *network* is used today in a wide range of domains. We talk of computer networks, radio and television networks, business networks, social networks, telecommunications networks, community networks, etc. The simplest definition of a network would be "an interconnected or interrelated group or system." Applied to the social or community field, it would become "a group of people who remain in contact for mutual support for the advancement of common goals."

In the computer world, a network can be made up of just a few computers connected with wires, or as we see with the Internet, it can be millions of computers located in various geographical areas that are connected together through phone lines, cables, or radio waves. This picture brings to mind the model of the apostolic network Paul established and the developments we see today in the second apostolic age.

Now, another interesting element for us can be found with wireless computer networking: the *base station*. The base station, which is a radio receiver/transmitter, is the real hub of the local wireless network, acting as a gateway between a wired network and the wireless network. I would link the function of a base station to that of an apostolic center, or as some people like to call it, an apostolic hub.

Let's take another look at Antioch and see how it qualified, ahead of Jerusalem, to be the base station for the early church's first apostolic network and how it developed from there.

THE INITIAL BASE STATION

When the time came to move ahead with the creation of multiple communities of believers spread out geographically and to link them in an apostolic network, the Holy Spirit chose Antioch as a base station. Why not Jerusalem?

The Problem with Jerusalem

Jerusalem was the apostolic seat of authority after Jesus returned to heaven. In that city, the eleven remaining original apostles were instructed to wait for the promise of the Father, the coming of the Holy Spirit, before they started on their mission to be witnesses of the resurrection of the Lord. While they were waiting, Peter told the disciples they needed to replace Judas with one of the men who had been with them for the last three years of ministry so that the person they chose could join them in witnessing of the resurrection of Jesus (see Acts 1:21–22). Clearly, they understood the mission they had, except Peter never mentioned the part Jesus had told them about taking their message *outside* Jerusalem.

When the Pentecost outpouring happened, Peter stood up with the eleven and declared to the crowd that what they were experiencing had been foretold by the prophet Joel (see Acts 2:16). So, the very first apostolic decree of the new era established the prophetic dimension. This is no surprise when we consider

Ephesians 2:20, which says the house of God was "built on the foundation of the apostles and prophets, with Christ Jesus himself as the chief cornerstone."

The important council of Jerusalem (see Acts 15) that happened roughly twenty years after Peter's initial discourse also indicates that the church in Jerusalem remained the apostolic seat of authority for many years.

However, there are no indications of any efforts made to preach the gospel outside Jerusalem until the persecution following Stephen's death occurred and "those who had been scattered preached the word wherever they went" (Acts 8:4). True, during that period of time, Philip went to Samaria (see Acts 8:5–13), followed by Peter and John (see Acts 8:14–25), and we see the church eventually spread throughout Judea, Galilee, and Samaria (see Acts 9:31), but what we don't see is a strategic plan to organize the churches into a functional network.

However, before we judge the apostles in Jerusalem for not initiating the apostolic network we could presume was needed, let me suggest that the political and economic situation of Jerusalem might have been the reason why the Holy Spirit chose another city, Antioch, to establish the first base station for the network that would soon touch the whole known world.

If we draw a parallel between an apostolic base and wireless technology, we can see that in order to have a good base station, certain requirements are necessary, mainly the capacity to provide a strong and fast connection without interruption. All users depend on the efficiency of the base station to be effectively linked together. Jerusalem was an apostolic center in terms of authority, but in terms of becoming a hub to link the nations, her situation was not ideal. The city was often in upheaval and revolt against Rome. Placed under trusteeship and watched by the Romans, Jerusalem was plagued by a disastrous economic situation.

Antioch, on the other hand, had the perfect profile to become the first base station for the expansion of Christianity with networks of churches. The Holy Spirit knew what He was doing when He sent men from the Jerusalem dispersion to travel "as far as Phoenicia, Cyprus and Antioch, spreading the word only among Jews" (Acts 11:19), then other men (in the course of the following years) from Cyprus and Cyrene to Antioch "to speak to Greeks also, telling them the good news about the Lord Jesus" (Acts 11:20). This gave way to a new type of church, with Jews and Gentiles worshipping together. That was so unique that the church of Jerusalem sent Barnabas to examine what had happened in Antioch (see Acts 11:22–23).

Antioch's Profile

Antioch was a rich commercial center at the crossing of the north-south and east-west trade routes. After Rome and Alexandria, it was the largest city of the Roman Empire, with a population of more than 500,000 people coming from a great number of nations. It was in Antioch that coins with the effigy of the Roman Emperor were made. When Jesus asked the Pharisees, "Show me the coin used for paying the tax…Whose image is this? And whose inscription?" (Matt. 22:19–20), they probably showed Him a coin that had been made in Antioch. Not only was Antioch a commercial city, but it was also a cultural and intellectual center that was much more dynamic than Jerusalem, being equipped with splendid temples, theatres, aqueducts, public baths, gardens, and fountains.

With its constant flow of visitors and business traffic, Antioch was in contact with all the important cities of the empire; it was an ideal location for a church that wanted to spread itself out to the nations.

The Jews were forming a great community in the city, but the separation between Jews and Gentiles was not as radical as in other places, which allowed, as we have seen, the creation of the first mixed church.

Antioch had a deep influence on Paul; not only did it become his home base and launching pad for more than twenty years of missionary trips, but with its cultural pool, it provided a fertile ground for Barnabas and Paul to open the church to the world of their time. The church of Antioch was the first church to move away from strict Judaism and to integrate Gentiles into their community. That, more than anything else, qualified Antioch to become the base station for the first apostolic network that was formed because there were no longer any ethnic barriers to hinder the church from expanding. However, the favorable socio-economic factors we have described were required first.

What am I saying? The Holy Spirit doesn't work in a vacuum. He works His plans and purposes inside a created world, using the convergence of natural conditions to facilitate the birth of spiritual realities.

Apostolic centers are not emerging randomly; it appears the Holy Spirit is locating them geographically in a strategic way that takes into account the presence of factors that will allow them to feed networks that will bring transformation to the world. Antioch met all the criteria to be such an apostolic center, as did Corinth and Ephesus after that. This is not to say that only a metropolis can foster apostolic centers, but I believe natural conditions conducive to operating as a base station are certainly welcome. Smaller towns can serve as a hub for remote regions, but the famous, "If you build it, he will come" from *The Field of Dreams,* doesn't necessarily apply to just any distant field.

THE TURNING POINT OF ACTS 15:36

We have already discussed the Acts 13 shift that sent Paul on his first apostolic trip. At that time, Barnabas was still the main apostolic leader in the picture. He had already played a major role in Paul's life by introducing him to Peter and James in Jerusalem and by calling him out of Tarsus to bring him to Antioch. This time, he led Paul into Cyprus, which was the country he knew best, as he was born there. As the trip continued, Paul's leadership was clearly established, and after a period of two years, they had successfully established pastoral churches in many cities of the empire. On their way back to Antioch, their sending base, they stopped for a second time at a few of the young churches and appointed elders, or pastors, to care for the flock.

They reported to the church of Antioch all the Lord had done during their travels and how He had opened a door of faith to the Gentiles (see Acts 14:27). That's all very good. However, this is still not what I would call a network. Having a growing number of churches was a positive step, but something else needed to happen in order to secure the future expansion of the kingdom of God. It must be understood that church planting alone, as beneficial as it might be, can never give the full measure of God's apostolic plan.

What was it, then, that was still missing? After going through the historic Council of Jerusalem, which sealed the entrance of the Gentiles in the faith, and after having spent considerable time in Antioch, Paul turned to Barnabas and said:

> Let us go back and visit the believers in all the towns where we preached the word of the Lord and see how they are doing (Acts 15:36).

"Let's go back and see how they're doing"—that was the turning point. That declaration signed the death warrant of scattered and isolated Christianity. From that moment on, networks of interconnected churches would become the structure that apostles would establish, with apostolic centers strategically situated as power relays to feed the links in all directions.

ON THE FOUNDATION OF APOSTLES AND PROPHETS

Paul eventually left for his second trip with Silas instead of Barnabas. That's interesting because Silas was a prophet (see Acts 15:32), but not only that, he was also a respected leader from Jerusalem (see Acts 15:22–27); he had come to Antioch with Judas, who was another prophet, as spokesmen for the Council of Jerusalem. So we have an apostle, Paul, and a prophet, Silas, traveling together to launch the networking phase of the apostolic mandate, which was to link the young churches Paul had established during his first trip into a relational network.

There were also prophets involved when Paul and Barnabas were first commissioned as apostles in Antioch (see Acts 13:1–3). It's important to realize how foundational apostles and prophets are in the kingdom of God (see Eph. 2:20). Otherwise, our networks, instead of being apostolically led and prophetically influenced, will end up being administratively led, giving birth to legal structures rather than flexible wineskins hosting new life.

THE INITIAL NETWORK

The first apostolic network definitely took shape with Paul's second trip. Before that, he was going from place to place preaching the good news, leading men to faith, and giving them basic instructions to continue after he left. His stays were rather short, and there's no indication he had any comprehensive plan for the future. However, when he declared at the start of his second trip, "Let us go back and see how they are doing," it is clear he was intentionally moving with a vision to link the churches in a relational net with sustained communication. To that effect, it was also during that period he started to write letters to churches (Galatians, 1 and 2 Thessalonians).

Besides visiting churches he had established during his first trip, Paul also saw two important developments take place. First, he enlarged his territory up to Macedonia and Greece. Then, he established a second apostolic center in Corinth and touched base with Ephesus, which would go on to become his third center a few years later. Both Corinth and Ephesus were, like Antioch, key socio-economic cities in their parts of the world. Paul's initial network then had base stations in the East with Antioch, in Asia with Ephesus, and in Greece with Corinth. Some might consider that there were other cities that hosted apostolic centers, and that's possible, but I think the three I just named were the most important ones.

So, what do we have for a basic model? A large territory, dozens of churches, and three strategically located apostolic centers.

EARLY APOSTOLIC EXPLOSION

Wheels within Wheels

When we look at the early expansion of the church across the Roman Empire, the term *apostolic explosion* is not exaggerated to describe the movement. It is one of the most amazing phenomena in history, especially if one considers that it started with a small band of unknown Jews from remote Jerusalem, a somewhat insignificant city as far as Rome was concerned.

There's no doubt Paul's role in this venture was central. On top of his systematic thinking and writing, he was gifted by the Holy Spirit to establish the structural model that linked the churches into an organic network that could challenge the Roman system.

However, it is important to see that Paul was not the only apostle moving and that there was not only one network, but rather a "wheels within wheels" network structure with multiple apostles at work.

Silas and Timothy

First, in Paul's own network we find Silas and Timothy, the companion apostles. The greeting opening the first letter to the Thessalonians is from the three men, Paul, Silas, and Timothy. Then Paul confirms they are apostles (see 1 Thess. 2:6). For Silas, that would make him both an apostle and a prophet. He shared with Paul the beatings and imprisonment in Philippi (see Acts 16:22–23) and the troubles in Thessalonica (see Acts 17:10), and Paul also trusted him to continue the work in his absence in Macedonia (see Acts 17:14; 18:5). Then, around fifteen years later, Silas worked in another network, this time with Peter (see 1 Pet. 5:12–13). We also have the example of Timothy, Paul's son in the faith, who travelled in many regions and had a season as residing apostle in Ephesus (see 1 and 2 Timothy).

Titus, Epaphroditus, Andronica, Junia, Priscilla, and Aquila

If we continue in Paul's sphere, Titus also functioned apostolically in Crete (see Titus 1:5), and a few others are named, like Epaphroditus, "my brother, fellow worker and fellow soldier, who is also your messenger [*apostolos*]" (Phil. 2:25). Then we find Andronicus and Junia. They had been in prison with Paul, and he viewed them as "outstanding among the apostles" (Rom. 16:7). Junia's mention is a strong argument in favor of women apostles, to which we could add Priscilla with her husband Aquila, who are not specifically counted as apostles but as Paul's co-workers (see Rom. 16:3). However, on top of showing a great autonomy in the apostolic mission, we see them mentoring another apostle, Apollos, in the ways of God (see Acts 18:26), which could be an indicator of apostolic gifting in them as well.

Apollos

This leads us to look at apostles who were not in direct alignment with Paul, like Apollos. When Aquila and Priscilla met Apollos in Ephesus, it is obvious Paul had not taught him. But after he received adjustment he needed in his theology, the brothers and sisters sent him to Achaia with a letter of recommendation, and he was a great help there (see Acts 18:27–28). He settled in the apostolic center Paul had established in Corinth and functioned there as an apostle. During that time, Paul arrived in Ephesus and started to lay the foundation for his third apostolic center.

In 1 Corinthians 4:6–9, Paul recognized Apollos as an apostle like him. However, Apollos was not aligned with Paul like Timothy and Silas were. This is the conclusion we can draw when we read that some people in Corinth were saying, "I follow Paul," and others were saying, "I follow Apollos" (1 Cor. 3:4). This in no way undermined the respect Paul had for Apollos, although he had to address the people for their wrong attitudes in this. Paul's deep consideration for Apollos was shown when he wrote, "I planted the seed, Apollos watered it, but God has been making it grow" (1 Cor. 3:6), and "For we are co-workers in God's service; you are God's field, God's building (1 Cor. 3:9). We thus have two apostles whose spheres overlapped without any competition. They both worked in God's field and retained the autonomy that corresponded to their calling. Sometime after Apollos first stayed in Corinth, Paul exhorted him to go back:

> Now about our brother Apollos: I strongly urged him to go to you with the brothers. He was quite unwilling to go now, but he will go when he has the opportunity (1 Cor. 16:12).

These strong personalities, men of vision, were able to respect the privilege of each other to discern God's will.

Barnabas and Mark

We don't hear much about Barnabas after his separation from Paul, but that doesn't mean he stopped being active as an apostle. What we know of Barnabas shows he was a strong apostle, used to travel. So when he left with Mark, also known as John, for Cyprus, as reported in Acts 15:39, we can conclude without hesitation that while Paul was launching his network with Silas, Barnabas was doing the same in other regions.

Approximately six years later, when Paul was defending his apostleship in his first letter to the Corinthians, he mentioned Barnabas as a reference, which indicates to us that his former companion was still well-respected and must have been actively working from his own sphere all those years (see 1 Cor. 9:5–6).

Another five years after that letter, we learn that Mark is now with Paul in Rome (see Col. 4:10), and three years later, with Peter (see 1 Pet. 5:13), showing the organic movement between the different apostolic spheres and networks.

Spheres

I mentioned the word *sphere* quite a few times in the last paragraphs. This is a concept we need to understand when it comes to networks. Paul had no hesitation to declare he had authority:

> So even if I boast somewhat freely about the authority the Lord gave us for building you up rather than tearing you down, I will not be ashamed of it (2 Cor. 10:8).

However, he specified that this was valid only within the limits of his own sphere and not beyond:

> We, however, will not boast beyond proper limits, but will confine our boasting to the sphere of service God himself has assigned to us, a sphere that also includes you (2 Cor. 10:13).

Each apostle has a sphere that God assigns to him or her. Within that sphere, the apostle has great authority, but outside of it, none, unless he or she is invited to come in. This is why in the developments of apostolic networks we need to walk humbly and avoid presumption. Apostles don't have authority to enter any place they want without the assignment of the Lord, and there must be a respect and deference for each other's field, whether it is a geographical territory or a spiritual one:

> Neither do we go beyond our limits by boasting of work done by others. Our hope is that, as your faith continues to grow, our sphere of activity among you will greatly expand, so that we can preach the gospel in the regions beyond you. For we do not want to boast about work already done in someone else's territory (2 Cor. 10:15–16).

The explosion of the first-century church saw more apostles

developing their spheres, more churches being planted, more centers being established, and more networks covering the regions and nations. How does this translate today?

A POWER GRID FOR TODAY

Today's Networks

Even if the times have changed, the original pattern is still relevant. *Apostolic networks present the most potent framework for sustaining the end-time activation of the kingdom dynamics.* But what do networks look like today?

At this relatively young stage of the second apostolic age, the development of networks is still new. What we have seen so far are mainly networks of churches, ministries, and leaders linked together through twenty-first century apostles and their teams. Most of the time these apostles have started out by developing a base station, an apostolic center that then becomes the hub around which their network gravitates. Some actually spend most of their time working from their apostolic center. They are residing apostles. In those cases, their network is usually strongly connected to the apostolic center. However, some others delegate most of the current leadership of the center to associates and have a travelling ministry. They are itinerant apostles. In those cases, the networks are often only remotely connected to the apostolic centers and gravitate more around the apostles themselves. And between those two ends of the spectrum, we find a variety of combinations with partly residing, partly itinerant apostles with networks that can take many shapes, vertical or horizontal, and serve diverse purposes.

World War II or Microsoft?

Now, I mentioned apostolic teams many times. Not all apostles work well with teams. Some are loners; they like to do their work by themselves. Others like to surround themselves with a team but nevertheless function in a top down structure of authority. Peter Wagner has a gift for finding the right terms to describe what he observes. He came up with the term *World War II Apostles* for those generals who like to work that way. They tend to be competitive and territorial. It's not that they are not true apostles—they are! It's just that sometimes you could almost hear Frank Sinatra sing, "I did it my way."

However, I'm sure that if you happen to know one of those apostles, chances are you would wholeheartedly testify to their character and integrity and love and endearing personality. They are leaders who have done exploits and accomplished phenomenal work for the kingdom. They just happen to represent a stage when the restoration of apostles was just starting and people were finding their way.

But over time, through trial and error, our understanding of the apostolic ministry has evolved and has given way to another generation of apostles whom Peter Wagner describes as *Microsoft Apostles*. You can readily see the picture in your mind. Those apostles love teamwork. They major on cooperation rather than competition; the borders of their spheres are not rigid, and actually they can function well in many spheres at the same time. You might find them humming, "With a Little Help from My Friends."

A New Type of Networks

With all the different styles, flavors, and generations of apostles we have, and with all the different expressions of networks we know, there is still a new type of network that needs to be established today, because it will fast track our progress in fulfilling the apostolic commission to invade, occupy, and transform this world with the kingdom of God. This new type of network will link apostolic centers to one another, producing *a power grid for territorial governance*.

Apostolic centers are powerhouses grounded in real life, strategically situated within a geographical territory, hosting the presence of the Lord, and invested with authority from above. They are heaven's headquarters on the earth.

However, we would make a huge mistake to think for one minute that they carry enough power to wage their own wars. Apostolic centers cannot afford the luxury of existing independently from one another; there is a reality bigger than any center can face alone, and global vision has to be a characteristic of the apostolic DNA that we carry.

It's easy to foresee a proliferation of apostolic networks happening in our day. Many more apostles are coming on the scene, with as many spheres of authority as the Lord allocates to them. They will form creative teams: teams of apostles, teams of prophets, teams of multi-gifted leaders, spheres intersecting with spheres, wheels within wheels. The shapes and forms may vary a lot and surprise us, but regardless of the variations, the church will remain established on the foundation of apostles and prophets, with Jesus Christ as the cornerstone, and the house of God will continue to be a habitation for God in the spirit. Wherever and however this house will be found, apostolic authority will continue to be in God's plan for it, and when these houses link together in spiritual relationship, we will see what kind of network God had in mind when He devised the plan for His spiritual temple on the earth.

Global Picture

Just as Antioch, Corinth, and Ephesus hosted resource centers for the growing number of churches in their parts of the world, in order to link together the net of churches and ministries that are to be wisely weaved inside the fabric of society, we need to see apostolic centers established in key cities in our nations, which will give the bread and the wine of the kingdom to the world.

These apostolic centers in the nations will work together to form a governing structure for the kingdom of God. Apostles will bring their networks together and will address the current issues we face. This will give birth to *networks of networks,* which will then form *global platforms* to host the authority of heaven in ever-increasing levels until Jesus comes again. This grid for governance will be based on the church mountain but will operate in all the other mountains of society as well. In this chapter, I'm mainly looking at the picture from the church domain, but in Chapter 9, I will expand on the impact of new apostolic centers operating in all the spheres of society.

FROM LEGAL TO RELATIONAL

The present change of wineskins is shifting us from legal structures to relational networks. We are used to hearing that the Christian faith is about relationship. If this is indeed the case, we need to ask ourselves why we have so often slipped into a legal mode with our practices. And we need to ask what a true relational *modus operandi* would look like. I cannot pretend to know all the answers to that one, but I do know the paradigms are shifting.

We all know how legal structures operate in the church. Like all other legal structures, they conform to the law, which is a set of prescribed rules enforced by authorities. The idea behind it all is to ensure the members within the structure believe and practice what is right. In order to achieve that, in-depth statements of faith and bylaws are written. Nothing is really wrong with that, except it is very hard to reduce life to a fixed number of rules to abide by. Jesus never took the legalistic approach to solve life's questions, and He didn't leave bylaws to run the church after He left, either. Of course, the Bible includes many guidelines for what to believe and how to live, but we must guard against turning it into a dry manual. The Father's intention was that His abiding Holy Spirit would guide us through the living Scripture and lead us into vibrant truth.

A legalistic mindset can be found at any level in the church. It's neither a matter of size nor of generation. A small house group can be plagued by a legalistic spirit just as much as a large organization can; a radical young adult ministry can be as rigid and controlling as a seniors' club. In traditional organizations, members will typically be asked to completely agree with a number of written or understood statements that reflect the organization's revelation and interpretation of God's requirements. Many times, the members will have to sign a paper to officially register their agreement. Again, nothing of that is wrong by itself, but many would say they felt hindered rather than released in those settings. How many times have people who have signed such documents afterward said something like, "Well, I don't really believe articles 12 and 14, but what could I do?"

The reality is we have been made with a desire to belong. The longing for companionship is certainly not limited to marriage alone. Add to this that as believers we also have a desire to respect authority and to be faithful in our commitments, and we start to understand that it's not easy to find our way, with a good conscience, around some of the legalist structures that are well-established in the Christian landscape.

I said "some" because, fortunately, not all organizations are legalistic; there are levels of freedom and life-giving ways in many fellowships. However, we are at a crossroads in the history of the church, and new wineskins are emerging.

Apostolic centers are certainly advanced outposts in that transition, and apostolic networks, on a larger scale, are also on the cutting edge of what the Holy Spirit is doing. However, we need to admit that even among the apostolic networks already established, it's possible to find some practices that reflect the old ways of doing things. In the same manner that the restoration of the apostles has been progressing through seasons of learning, apostolic networks are also in constant evolution. They are becoming more and more organic and relational, and the apostles leading them are becoming more like healthy fathers with their families rather than CEOs with their businesses.

In those networks, we speak of alignment rather than covering. We value heart-to-heart dialogue, done with respect, rather than having battles to impose our views. We need a willingness to walk in the alignment proposed. In such apostolic networks, there is space for members to think for themselves and hear and obey the

Lord's instructions. And there's room to agree to disagree. I'm not talking here about the basic tenets of the Christian faith as found in Scripture. Those are non-negotiable. But on the subjects that are matters of interpretation or opinion, you will find leaders, even at the highest levels, who hold differing views but are nonetheless walking together in close unity. That is a sign of maturity and love that the world needs to see in us.

Apostolic networks are to become the expression of the prayer of Jesus in John 17: "That they may be one." When we come closer to such a unity, it testifies of the victory of Jesus activated in His body. This is the living structure that can release the grace of God on the earth and disciple the nations.

BUILDING PROTOTYPES

Building a prototype is never easy. It's like assembling a puzzle without having the picture in front of us as we work. It's a work for pioneers. We're building something we have envisioned, but for the people watching us from the sidelines, what we are doing is not always obvious. In real life, that can even translate into resistance and opposition.

For the early church, they had to face the spirit of the religious structure of their day. What they were building was a threat to the established religion of their fathers. In our day, apostolic networks can also be perceived as a threat to the traditional church structure. That's unfortunate, but it again verifies the statement Jesus made that we can't pour new wine into old wineskins (see Matt. 9:17).

On the other hand, once you succeed in building a viable prototype, the promises of reproduction are phenomenal. That's why the enemy resists our efforts so much when he knows we are breaking through new ground. The apostolic centers and the networks linking them are the latest prototypes to be developed in the church. We will soon be able to start exporting them to help the whole body. I often say to friends that, in just a few years, the reality of apostolic centers and networks will have become the norm, not the exception. That's the power of prototypes appearing at the right time in history.

TERRITORIAL GOVERNANCE FOR KINGDOM ADVANCEMENT

I wrote in Chapter 1 that there's no life without structure. Now, we know the words of Jesus are spirit and life (see John 6:33). That has never been in question, at least among believers; we all agree His message carries spiritual life. The question we have been struggling with is, *How do we host this life so it can continue to grow and be made available to a hungry world?* So again, our challenge is with the wineskin, so that the precious wine will not be spilled.

An incredible number of books and sermons have been written and preached to help individuals become godly vessels for the presence of God, but fewer on how to collectively be a responsible and mature body that can disciple cities and nations into the abundant life. However, the concept that wineskins convey is much more collective than individual because it's in a cluster of grapes that the juice is found, not in individual grapes (see Isa. 65:8). Since this is the case, we should adopt a global view on the mandate of the church, which is apostolic in nature, and look for the structures that will best serve that mandate.

In Matthew 28:19, Jesus told us to "make disciples of all nations." Some people, though, have a hard time seeing that this word could really apply to nations. Yet we know Revelation 11:15 needs to be fulfilled:

> The kingdom of the world has become the kingdom of our Lord and of his Messiah, and he will reign for ever and ever.

For the same people, this means the reign of Jesus on the earth not only belongs to the future, but we, as believers, should not even work toward that goal now, leaving it to Him (and to Him alone) to establish His kingdom when He comes. Not only that, but some have come to the conclusion that while we know this reign will come and we will be part of it, it would be wrong on our part to aim for it before Jesus comes again.

The option left to the church, still according to the same view, would be to bring the greatest possible number of souls to salvation, but without trying to touch the structures of society, this being left for Jesus Himself to do in the future. In other words, until Jesus comes again, our only option is to snatch individual souls out of the enemy's hand, one by one, without trying to stop the devil from reigning on the earth.

However, on the other hand, if we consider that in order to fulfill our commission to disciple nations we need to touch all areas of society with a brand new system of values, then we will have to put in place new wineskins corresponding to freshly rediscovered biblical paradigms: a new spiritual structure of governance led by the Holy Spirit, bringing transformation to the world.

This is what we will explore in the next chapter.

PART 3

Establishing Alignment for Territorial Transformation

CHAPTER 9
Transforming the Present Day

CONTENTION FOR TERRITORIAL DOMINION

Paul's preaching brought a great harvest of souls, and his teaching trained scores of disciples and still continues to do so. But he didn't stop there; he openly challenged the rule of Satan in all levels of society and laid a base for the transformation of the cities and nations he was sent to. The clearest example of this can be seen in the events that transpired during the three years Paul spent in Ephesus, on his third apostolic trip.

Strategic Location of Ephesus

Capital of the province of Asia, Ephesus was a very important political, commercial, and religious center. Paul decided the city was a key location for an apostolic center that would be a hub for the territories he had already evangelized. It was an equal distance from Galatia and Thessalonica, 400 kilometers away from Corinth, and about the same from Philippi and Pisidian Antioch. From Ephesus, Paul could send and receive letters and messengers from all the churches he had established.

During that period, Paul reached the height of his apostolic activity. His influence impacted the whole province, and history tells us many political leaders and businessmen had established relationships with him. It was in Ephesus that "God did extraordinary miracles through Paul, so that even handkerchiefs and aprons that had touched him were taken to the sick, and their illnesses were cured and the evil spirits left them" (Acts 19:11–12).

However, that activity did not make everybody happy, and Paul, after writing to the Corinthians that "a great door for effective work" had opened for him, added, "and there are many who oppose me" (1 Cor. 16:9). But this time, instead of coming from the religious Jews from the synagogue, the opposition came from a whole different direction: the merchants from the temple of the goddess Artemis.

A Pagan World Center

Ephesus was the world center for the cult devoted to Artemis, or Diana for the Romans. Pilgrims came from everywhere to visit her temple—one of the Seven Wonders of the World—and to celebrate by the thousands the huge annual festival that took place in May, the month dedicated to the goddess. The temple housed a crowd of priests, eunuchs, and prostitutes and drew numerous magicians, comedians, musicians, fortunetellers, and astrologers. Further, Ephesus was quite the market for silver shrines, reproductions of the temple, and this lucrative business provided jobs to a large number of silversmiths and craftsmen.

Ephesus was the seat of one of the most powerful deities of antiquity, a territorial spirit that had a hold on the social and economic life of all Asia and beyond. That's what we would call a principality's stronghold; it was a world center for witchcraft and idolatry. Nevertheless, this was exactly where God chose to send Paul to display His great power and authority.

Setting the Stage

The confrontation developed in three stages. Firstly, individuals were delivered from evil spirits that had afflicted them (see Acts 19:12).

Secondly, many who practiced witchcraft brought their books and burned them publicly. The value of those books was estimated to be fifty thousand drachmas, which is around ten thousand dollars. That day was a huge blow to the enemy's stronghold. The narrative of this event concludes with, "In this way the word of the Lord spread widely and grew in power" (Acts 19:20). Thirdly, Paul persuaded and turned many people away from idolatry, not only in Ephesus but in practically the whole province of Asia, saying man-made gods were not gods at all (see Acts 19:26). This last point is what triggered the incident we refer to as the Riot in Ephesus and depicts the reality of territorial spheres of authority in a vivid way.

The Riot

Demetrius, an influential business owner in the silver shrine industry, seeing the threat Paul's activity represented to his trade, called on his fellow craftsmen. After they gathered to hear what Demetrius had to say, they started to cry out and succeeded in troubling the whole city, who then rushed to the theater, which had a capacity of 25,000 people. This gives us an idea of how many craftsmen there must have been in order to produce such an uproar and the strength of that economic sector in Ephesus.

The hysterical way the crowd shouted the name of the goddess for two hours is quite revealing. This outburst of rage was fueled by much deeper concerns than the economic losses of a declining pagan temple industry. It was a direct response to the territorial advance of the kingdom of God. Demetrius himself had stated it plainly:

> There is danger not only that our trade will lose its good name, but also that the temple of the great goddess Artemis will be discredited; and *the goddess herself, who is worshiped throughout the province of Asia and the world, will be robbed of her divine majesty* (Acts 19:27, emphasis added).

The apostolic center Paul had established in Ephesus had become an unbearable challenge to the spiritual forces based in that area. The whole riot was nothing but a staged contention for territorial dominion.

Beyond Religion

This incident shows that the furthering of the kingdom of God is not simply a religious matter; it touches other spheres of society as well and can provoke social debates with economic repercussions. It is a military operation in the spirit to destroy the works of the devil and to bring transformation to the world with God's love, mercy, power, and authority.

DIVIDED WE CAN'T OVERCOME

> Every kingdom divided against itself will be ruined, and every city or household divided against itself will not stand (Matt. 12:25).

There are no two ways around this one. To gain spiritual authority in any region, you need cohesion in the camp. That's what Jesus was explaining with the tragic fate of every kingdom or household divided against itself. To make sure we would understand, He explained it again in verses 29–30, this time using the image of a strong man, his house, and his goods. Here's my interpretation of this passage:

> In order to have enough strength to overcome the strong man, move into the territory where he has set his rule, take his goods (which are the precious lives of the people he has enslaved), set them free, and give them back all their possessions, we will have to stop our selfish pursuits of ministry and unite together as one with Jesus.

If we want to see whole areas conquered, occupied, and transformed, we need to strategically move away from the sad ending of the Book of Judges, when there was no king in Israel, and link the apostolic centers and networks under the leadership of the one and only King, the Lord Jesus Christ. This remains, above anything else, the greatest task of the apostles in our day and age.

DYSFUNCTIONAL HISTORY

In those days Israel had no king; everyone did as they saw fit (Judg. 21:25).

The last sentence of the Book of Judges is both a summary of the tribulations of Israel in the period following the conquest of the Promised Land and a prophetic picture of the church after the first apostolic age.

In those days, Israel literally had no human king, which explains why everyone did as they saw fit. This is not to say there was no revelation of God's will, for He had given them the Torah. But a law without a king is just as good as a king without a law. However, the truth of the matter is that even if they didn't have a human king, God was their King (as with the church)—but sadly they had a hard time obeying their divine King. So, Israel repeatedly returned to sin, provoking God's anger and falling into the hands of their enemies (see Judg. 2:11–14). But because God is faithful to His covenants, every time that happened He would raise up judges, who were like temporary kings, and those judges gathered enough men to deliver the people from those who plundered them (see Judg. 2:16) and bring peace back to the land.

The church, on the other hand, does have a King who rules through the Holy Spirit, but when we look through the centuries past up to now, we have to conclude that for long periods in history, and even in our circles today, many have done as they saw fit rather than as the Lord desired. Instead of giving birth to the kingdom of God, we generated Christendom, which historically ruled by force or imposition over populations, a tragic perversion of man's original mandate to rule the earth (see Gen. 1:28). Nowadays, the failure of this religious system has become more and more obvious, leaving a fractured church in its wake.

DYSFUNCTIONAL OUTCOME

The outcome of having a church history where everyone has done as they saw fit, rather than submitting to the voice of one King, is tragic. Instead of advancing with order and efficiency, we have become a dysfunctional body of believers trying to fulfill a mission that is way beyond our grasp. The nations are watching the pathetic attempts of divided members trying to achieve what only coordinated efforts will ever have a chance of accomplishing. Without the proper linking of apostolic centers and networks, no global structure will be in place to implement the orders of King Jesus with strategic efficiency.

Instead of a fit and well-proportioned body, we end up with a few supersized ministries that are poorly connected to a weak and random collection of scattered local churches. Viewed from heaven, we must be a sad picture of a deformed body barely connected to its head.

That's most assuredly the number one reason why—in spite of all our efforts, energy, and money—we have been so limited in our capacity to produce measurable transformation in the nations with the gospel of the kingdom. The problem has not been the resistance of the enemy or the lack of workers but our own anarchy in the way we do church.

Fortunately, we are living in the times of the restoration of all things (see Acts 3:21), and the Holy Spirit is leading the church back to the divine government He implemented in the days of Acts.

THE NEW GOVERNMENT OF ACTS

It seemed good to the Holy Spirit and to us... (Acts 15:28).

The adventure of the church had started well: Jews bringing the gospel to other Jews. Yes, persecutions came to shake the early believers, but as far as understanding their mission and moving forward, the matter was at least simple. They were working on familiar ground within their culture, viewing *the Way* as a development of the faith of their fathers (see Acts 24:14). The government of the church was in the hands of the apostles and consisted mainly in establishing the right priorities and responding to the spiritual and logistical needs of a growing community, like we see in the decision to appoint men to serve at the tables, leaving the apostles free to pray and teach the word of God (see Acts 6:2–4).

However, something was coming that would rock their world in a dramatic way and require the government of the church to operate in a whole new dimension: the Gentiles started to get saved.

The Jews didn't know what to do with them. When Jesus told them they would be His witnesses "to the ends of the earth" (Acts 1:8), they probably thought He meant they would go to the Diaspora, to the Jewish communities scattered throughout the earth. Seeing the Gentiles coming to join with them was more than a shock; they had no point of reference in their paradigm for this new turn of events.

Some thought they should accept them as is, while others insisted they needed to be circumcised, meaning they had to adopt Judaism to follow the Lord. Since this was starting to create confusion and quarrels, they called the historic council of Jerusalem to find a solution. After much discussion, James stood up and gave a revelatory word: The Gentiles coming to faith was the fulfillment of God's promise to restore the tent of David!

Finally they decided the Gentiles wouldn't have to be circumcised, which was one of the most important governmental decrees ever to be made by the church in all its history, prior to and after that council. It forever sealed the full entrance of the Gentiles into the church and paved the way for the creation of the one new man later described in Ephesians 2:15.

But the most astounding shift, which went even beyond that defining moment, happened when the council wrote the opening of the letter they sent to announce their decision: "It seemed good to the Holy Spirit and to us..." (Acts 15:28). That ushered in a whole new level of spiritual governance that was needed for the council to make a historic decision of this magnitude. That type of spiritual government is what the Lord is restoring in the present day with the New Apostolic Reformation.

It is an awesome, unfathomable privilege on earth for people to be able to say, "The Holy Spirit and us," for in this lies the true secret of the authority to exercise dominion on the earth on behalf of our Father. As the apostolic networking continues to take place, we will keep moving away from the end of the Book of Judges and become better and more tangible expressions of the kingdom of God.

THE GREAT APOSTOLIC TASK: ALIGN EVERYTHING UNDER ONE KING

The level of authority the Lord is ready to share with His church in our day and age is absolutely staggering. If it wasn't for the unshakeable certitude that this authority is intended to be exercised on the earth, I would say it is out of this world! It could even be a scary thing to think mere humans can be made partakers of God's authority. Even if it is through delegation, this is still no ordinary power to handle. Apostles, in particular, are the first in line to be trusted with such an authority.

Knowing the danger that power and authority can represent when they fall into the wrong hands (the repercussions of that have unfortunately been felt many times over the course of human history), it is imperative for the apostolic movement to have holy hands and build only according to God's heart and plan. There ought to be no room for self-appointed apostles who desire to build their own kingdom for personal gain: "For such people are false apostles, deceitful workers, masquerading as apostles of Christ" (2 Cor. 11:13).

The high and holy task given to us demands that apostles conform to what Paul declared about himself. After opening chapter 9 of his first letter to the Corinthians with "Am I not free? Am I not an apostle?" he declared in verse 19, "I have made myself a slave to everyone..." (1 Cor. 9:19). And about his position with the Lord, he said he was "Paul, the prisoner of Christ Jesus" (Eph. 3:1). All is for Him, all is by Him, and all is through Him—the house, the bride, the kingdom, and all things. He must be first in everything and rule over everything. Knowing this, we ought to link apostolic centers and networks under the leadership of that one and only King.

This will lead to a functional rearrangement of the decision mechanisms, and that will require much more than the occasional apostolic round table discussion. We are talking here of apostles respecting each other's spheres (see 2 Cor. 10:13–18), honoring one another above themselves (see Rom. 12:10), and fulfilling the prayer of Jesus that we may be one (see John 17:21).

When spheres are coming together, when apostolic centers are being linked, when networks are joining with one another, then we can start talking about a global apostolic alignment with heaven and about territorial transformation becoming possible. Apostles need to link themselves together in an organic way, bringing not only their resources but also their hearts to the table.

TYPES OF UNITY

The church is used to certain levels of unity, and each of these levels requires different types of involvement. Here are a few of the most common types:

Mutual Benefit Unity
This is the "it's good for us and it's good for you, so let's do it"

unity. An example of this would be the sharing of resources when mutually beneficial. For example, you need a place to hold your church services, and we need some extra money. You can use our sanctuary on Sunday afternoons for a reasonable offering, and that offering will help us with our utility bill.

Common Goal Unity

We might invite a big-name evangelist to come to town. We pull together a number of churches to organize it and share the cost, and then we distribute the new people who are saved during the event among our various churches.

Fellowship Unity

It's nice to get together and share what we're doing, hear the latest news, and pray for one another as fellow servants of the Lord. That's a classic picture of many ministerial groups, where city pastors and leaders get together once a month or even more often than that. There is a level of friendship and mutual appreciation there, and at times, the prayer for the city can get quite intense. This is also the platform to organize the annual Christmas dinner or to talk about the plan for Easter. Nothing is wrong with this. That's all good. Our church has been hosting these monthly meetings for many years, as well as lending our sanctuary for the annual Christmas dinner. I love it!

Crisis Unity

This is when a crisis situation occurs and demands a heart response. There is no time to consider our differences. It may be a fire that left a neighborhood devastated or a natural disaster that hit the town (or maybe even the other side of the planet). Humanitarian relief is urgently needed, and we quickly respond.

Strategic Unity

This type of unity is for a moral fight that requires our involvement.

It might be to make presentations to the government or to take a public stand on an issue. In those circumstances, the numbers matter. Churches will come together, just for that time, even if they would normally not mingle together, being at the opposite ends of the Christian spectrum. That's strategic unity.

APOSTOLIC UNITY: THE KEY TO THE KINGDOM

The short list I just gave does not pretend to be an exhaustive presentation of the unity that we commonly see in regular church life—far from it. There are layers and layers of unity, ranging from the most superficial types to the deepest levels. But where am I going with this? I believe the apostolic government needed to bring transformation to our cities and nations is calling for a particular type of unity that is yet to come. Let's look into what that might be.

It would be wrong to say apostolic unity doesn't exist at all, but I would say we have not seen it in any consistent or lasting way. The reason for this may be the relatively young age of the New Apostolic Reformation. Apostles had to rediscover the old pathways, adapt them to our present age, and basically build from scratch. There was not much time, energy, or resources left to explore the land beyond one's own sphere. However, after having solidified the definition and existence of apostles, we are now entering the phase of the apostolic centers, which is providing a larger base of operations, with the result being that we will be able to wrestle with global issues. *Apostolic unity translates into governmental authority.*

Apostles have received a specific mission and need to have exemplary character, as we saw with Paul, who made himself the servant of all. Apostolic unity will carry that same DNA; it will remain functional, strategic, and visionary, while mirroring the attitude of Jesus:

Who, being in very nature God, did not consider equality with God something to be used to his own advantage;

rather, he made himself nothing by taking the very nature of a servant, being made in human likeness. And being found in appearance as a man, he humbled himself by becoming obedient to death—even death on a cross (Phil. 2:6–8).

Apostles will share a same love, being one in spirit and purpose, doing nothing out of selfish ambition or vain conceit, but in humility will consider others better than themselves, not looking only to their own interests but also to the interests of others (see Phil. 2:2–4). This will constitute, in line with Jesus' example, our path of obedience and death to self.

What will be the outcome of walking in such a way? For Jesus, the result was:

God exalted him to the highest place and gave him the name that is above every name, that at the name of Jesus every knee should bow, in heaven and on earth and under the earth, and every tongue acknowledge that Jesus Christ is Lord, to the glory of God the Father (Phil. 2:9–11).

That passage definitely carries the sense that God has already exalted Christ and that the fruits of that exaltation are continuing both now and in the future. I love the description of this in Daniel 7:14:

He was given authority, glory, and sovereign power; all nations and peoples of every language worshiped him. His dominion is an everlasting dominion that will not pass away, and his kingdom is one that will never be destroyed.

So, we can say this reign of Christ has already been established and continues to be extended. Now, let us give the second part of the answer to the question I asked. What will be the outcome for us if we pattern apostolic unity after the humble and obedient walk of Jesus?

But the people of the Most High will receive the kingdom and will possess it forever—yes, for ever and ever (Daniel 7:18).

OUR GLOBAL MANDATE TO TRANSFORM CULTURES

Let's take another look at our mandate. I titled this chapter "Transforming the Present Day." The question is, Are we really supposed to change the world, or should we limit our action to saving souls? In other words, why did Jesus come?

The Kingdoms of the World

I'd like to start with the third temptation Jesus faced. After trying twice, and failing, to insert a doubt in Jesus' mind about His identity as the Son of God, Satan went for the big win: "If You bow down and worship me, I'll give You the kingdoms of the world and their glory" (see Matt. 4:8–9). Satan was saying, "I know why You came and what You want, and You know what I always wanted. Let's make a deal."

Of course Jesus refused, not only because He will never worship His enemy but also because it was a fool's bargain. If Jesus would have accepted the deal, He would have gained the rule of the world but lost His union with the Father. The question of who receives the worship is definitely the clincher. In his desperate attempt to finally receive worship, Satan threw the most appealing carrot he could find: the kingdoms of the world.

Satan Robbed the Bank

We must not think Jesus brushed the third temptation off as an offer that presented no interest to Him. If that had been the case, Satan wouldn't have used it as his prime bait. It is also important to note that Jesus never contested whether the devil did indeed have the kingdoms of the world under his rule and could hand them out at will.

How did the devil gain authority over the earth? He did it by gaining authority over Adam (see Gen. 3:13; Eph. 2:2), who had received the mandate from God to rule the earth (see Gen. 1:28). When that happened, not only did man lose his authority, but God was robbed of worship as the Most High above all creation and of His reign through man over the earth.

Jesus Got It Back

When the time was right, Jesus came from heaven, was born of a virgin, and proceeded with His task to "destroy the devil's work" (1 John 3:8) and "to seek and to save what was lost" (Luke 19:10). What was the main work of the devil? Causing people to sin in order to enslave them. What was lost? God's government of the earth through man. But Jesus came to turn the tables and return honor to His Father. God could have taken the earth by force in the blink of an eye any time He wanted, but instead He chose to strip Satan of his authority through the same door the serpent had insidiously entered—the hearts of people.

The first Adam had willingly given away the dominion of the earth; the second Adam took it back by His obedient sacrifice, opening the door to every person who would believe to join and reign with Him on the earth (see 2 Tim. 2:10; Rev. 5:12). In this regard, our redemption gives us more than Adam ever had, for he had *fellowship* with God, whereas we have *union* with Him.

New Administration

The victory Christ secured at the cross, at the price of His shed blood, formed the basis for a new government to rule the earth. Let's put together just a few things Jesus told us:

You are the salt of the earth (Matt. 5:13).

You are the light of the world (Matt. 5:14).

Go and make disciples of all nations (Matt. 28:19).

Go into all the world and preach the good news to all creation (Mark 16:15).

Earth, world, nations, creation—these are global words for a global mandate, all conveying the concept of territorial transformation.

Reformation Time

It would be an incredible feat to succeed in explaining how this mandate could apply only to our private lives and not our public lives, or to say it only concerns the state of our souls and not the state of our nations. True, there is a difference between the private and public domains. However, should there not be an overflow of our personal faith into our public activities? Is this not what Jesus meant by "You are the salt of the earth" and "You are the light of the world"?

Without falling into the extreme of having governments led by religious groups, we need to look for the best way to bring the influence of the kingdom of God to all spheres of society in full respect of man's dignity and free will.

By bringing an influence, I mean affecting the spiritual atmosphere people live under by releasing the atmosphere of heaven. The spiritual atmosphere in any given location is a direct expression of the prevailing culture, which itself is the expression of the current values and beliefs that form people's paradigms. Paradigms then give birth to structures, and in the end these structures rule society, either by facilitating the flow of life or, in the worst-case scenarios, by quenching it completely.

Our mandate, as an apostolic people, is to do everything we can so the life of the Lord Jesus Christ will be constantly released on the earth in greater and greater measures without any hindrances or interruptions. In order to do that, we need to penetrate the culture of our day with the values and beliefs of the kingdom and renew the current paradigms so we start living the right way.

But where should we start?

THE STRENGTH OF THE SEVEN MOUNTAINS

In order to know where we should start if we want to influence cultures, it is helpful to ask ourselves: Where are mindsets formed?

In 1975, Bill Bright, founder of Campus Crusade, and Loren Cunningham, founder of Youth With A Mission (YWAM), had lunch together and compared lists they had each written separately of what they thought were the most influential spheres in society. They came up with basically the same list of seven areas: religion, family, education, government, media, arts and entertainment, and business. This sociological view of the culture-shapers or mind-molders is commonly known as the Seven Mountains Model, and over the last ten years it has been gaining more and more acceptance as a valid model, largely due to the brilliant presentations of a man named Lance Wallnau.

The Seven Mountains Model simply states that each of those spheres has a power of influence to mold the minds of people and shape the cultures and sub-cultures of society. The higher you climb on any given mountain, the more influence you gain in that particular sphere. At the very top, a very small number of people can have enough influence to shift the direction of entire nations.

We have seen in different nations that, in a relatively short time, small but well-organized groups have succeeded in shifting practices and laws by strategically gaining access to top positions on the right mountains. The changes they were able to bring came about even if the majority of the population was not of the same persuasion as they were. Abortion and gay marriage lobbies would be good examples of that in some of the western countries. Not stopping with just getting legislation changed, those lobby groups, from their positions of influence on mountaintops, are progressing toward shifting the mindsets of large segments of the population, creating a new global culture.

If we want to bring the influence of the kingdom of God to transform society, we cannot stay ignorant of those dynamics. As I was reflecting on the way the Seven Mountains are shaping our society, I realized the real impact they have is not so much dependent on the height or strength of any single one of them taken individually but rather on the singleness of purpose that links them into a *mountain range.*

Let's look again at the successful strategy of the proponents of abortion and gay marriage. First, they simultaneously invaded two of the seven mountains: media and arts and entertainment. By *invade* I mean they secured strong voices on both mountains, i.e. popular artists, popular sitcoms, regular coverage in the news for their public declarations. They linked the tops of those two mountains, which made their collective voice stronger than the isolated voice of either of the two. Then they succeeded in having like-minded candidates elected to governments, as well as in winning the ear of key members in the parties. They were few, but they had a voice—the government sphere, a third mountain linked to the first two. We could now consider it a mountain range standing strong for a common goal. And it goes on, adding one mountaintop after another to form a growing and longer mountain range. It is no wonder such an operation continues to produce the global shift we are now seeing. We would be wise to learn something from this.

MIGRATIONS FROM THE CHURCH MOUNTAIN: APOSTOLIC COLONIES ON THE OTHER MOUNTAINS

If we want the kingdom of God to grow in our nations, does it mean the religion mountain must have preeminence over the other mountains? I don't think so. Historically, it usually has not been a good thing when the religion mountain has dominated in society, Christian or not. Lots of abuses are reported when religion becomes institutionalized and rules over the affairs of people.

Many Christians entertain the dream of revival. In their minds, this means an intense season of activity in the church, characterized by massive conversions and explosive meetings. The only problem with that is revivals don't usually last very long and rarely succeed in producing lasting transformation in society. In other words, dreaming of a return to a golden age for the church mountain is not the way forward.

Traditionally, we have held a wrong concept of the kingdom of God. We are so used to camping on the church mountain that we believe everything else needs to gravitate around it. Not so. The kingdom of God is much bigger than the church, and the message of Jesus needs to be expressed and applied to all spheres of society, not only within the parameters of the local churches. In fact, this paradigm of seeing the church as the prime target for the gospel has been what has hindered us the most from fulfilling the great commission Jesus gave us and from bringing the gospel out of our walls to impact the world. The church should instead be viewed as the first base of operations for the kingdom, its equipping and sending force—its headquarters.

As the apostolic paradigm continues to develop, we will see more and more apostolic centers established, and from those centers, apostolic teams will be sent to the other mountains to bring the influence of the kingdom of God. This migration of apostolic teams will establish kingdom colonies on all mountains and trigger the process of transformation.

Our goal, then, is not to see how the church mountain can grow bigger for its own sake but how the church mountain can be more efficient in sending trained and equipped people to all the spheres of society. We have to stop trying to have everyone leave their mountain and come live on ours. This has never worked, and that's not about to change.

What we need to do is start training and empowering believers to rise up within the business sphere, in the decision-making tables of education, in the family-shaping councils, in the political arena, in the world of media, and in the wild jungle of arts and entertainment—people of vision, character, and faith. They are to be sent from the church mountain, to which they will remain organically connected, but their fields of ministry will not be on the religion mountain itself.

When I say ministry, I mean global transformational ministry. I am not talking here about people in the marketplace sharing their faith with colleagues and winning them to the Lord. This is an essential part of it and will always be so, but there is a bigger picture to consider here as well. I am talking about gaining a place of influence on the mountaintops where decisions are made that will affect the lives of our nations for generations to come.

As the church mindset starts to shift in that direction, creating a new paradigm, we will see new structures being formed. That's inevitable. New paradigms always give birth to new structures.

NEW BREEDS OF APOSTOLIC CENTERS

We are so used to operating within the sphere of religion that our minds don't see past those familiar boundaries. However, let me suggest that as apostolic centers continue to develop, not only will we keep sending more and more gifted individuals to exercise a growing influence on specific mountains, but we will also see the emergence of whole new breeds of centers, linked to the church mountain they were sent from, but based and operating on the other mountaintops.

It's hard to accurately describe what has not yet been manifested, but I have a vision of small apostolic teams starting to operate within different spheres of society and gradually gaining traction. According to the dynamics inherent to each sphere, specific structures will grow from the apostolic life released, and operational bases will emerge to facilitate the flow of that life. The Holy Spirit will give birth to centers that have been strategically configured to be relevant and efficient within each sphere. The impact of the gospel of the kingdom will be maximized, and transformation will occur.

Imagine, for example, such apostolic centers operating on the business mountain, resulting in new work ethics that could change the lives of whole segments of the world's population. It could mean the end of abusive production that uses children and women as working slaves. It could bring an end to industries releasing toxic waste that damages both nature and people. It could mean a redistribution of wealth and eradication of poverty. The possibilities are endless.

The business world seems to be one of the spheres that is the most ready to receive a new expression of apostolic centers today. Arts and entertainment is another sphere where we see developments in terms of Christian expression that could quickly lead to apostolic outposts. However, we should be ready to strategize for a migration of teams to *all* mountains, with an open mind to discover the new wineskins the Lord wants to birth.

NEW MOUNTAIN RANGES

Once apostolic centers have been established and are operating on the various mountains, linking them into networks will give a lot of leverage to bringing transformation to society. These networks will operate like the networks we have on the church mountain, but two things will be new: the unique features of the apostolic centers that will correspond to the specific mountains and the cross-connections between different mountaintops, rather than the one-dimensional model we are so familiar with on the church mountain.

When we lay out the Seven Mountains Model, we simplify reality to serve the purpose of giving everyone a broad picture— seven mountains with seven mountaintops.

The fabric of society is, of course, much more complex than that. Within each sphere of influence, there are numerous and diversified areas. For example, the entire business world is not led by just one corporation. It's a complex system with different clans and families, different sectors of economy, different markets, and different rules. The business mountain is, in reality, made up of many mountains with peaks reaching different heights. And the same is true for all of the other mountains. Education is not made up of only one teaching and learning philosophy; media does not operate the same everywhere; governments are the expression of different models of society, and so on and so forth. Even in nature, mountain ranges are not aligned as neat, single mountaintops, situated one after the other in an orderly fashion. From a bird's eye view, they are usually an interwoven landscape formed by a multitude of tops and valleys.

The apostolic strength will be deployed to invade these complex mountain ranges and occupy them with apostolic centers. The atmosphere of the kingdom of God will be released, and despite many conflicts and enormous challenges, the spiritual landscape will start to change because of the perseverance of the saints and the assistance of the Holy Spirit. New mountain ranges will appear, permeating all the sectors of our lives.

Healthy apostolic families will populate the nations, while prophetic companies will be found travelling from mountaintop to mountaintop, looking for the heavenly blueprints. I can foresee councils of apostles linked to one another, using those blueprints to launch global implementation operations on every mountain, redeeming the time, setting the captives free, and reshaping our cultures.

As we align ourselves with this cohesive and collective apostolic leadership, entire regions and nations will be restructured and transformed, and every single desire of our King will be fulfilled. In synergy the gifts will operate with focus and efficiency, expressing God-ordained governmental authority.

And then what? The time will come when the whole earth will be filled with the knowledge of the glory of the Lord (see Hab. 2:14).

TERRITORIAL TRANSFORMATION

There are many forces competing for the spheres of influence in this world—many alliances, many mountain ranges—waging for wealth and power. However, mountains that once rose in iniquity can also be brought low before the Lord's company:

What are you, O mighty mountain? Before Zerubbabel you will become level ground… (Zach. 4:7).

At the same time, another mountain will rise:

> In the last days the mountain of the Lord's temple will be established as the highest of the mountains; it will be exalted above the hills, and all nations will stream to it. Many peoples will come and say, "Come, let us go up to the mountain of the Lord" (Isa. 2:2–3).

I don't believe the mountain of the Lord is the mountain of religion. My conviction is that it represents the penetration of the kingdom of God into each of the seven mountains at the same time. It is the establishment of the apostolic centers that we've talked about, releasing the holy presence of the Lord and His government over all the mountains.

The mountain of the Lord is the habitation of God among people. It's the promise of the age to come, invading and transforming the present day. And there will be no peak so high or valley so low that people will be separated from "the kingdom of the Son he loves" (Col. 1:13).

That is why we are moved by the same spirit that Caleb had when he said to Joshua, "Now give me this hill country that the Lord promised me" (Josh. 14:12). The hour has come. It is already here.

> No longer will they teach their neighbor, or say to one another, "Know the Lord," because they will all know me, from the least of them to the greatest (Heb. 8:11).

I can live for that.

CONCLUSION

When I was about nine or ten, I wanted to have a Mustang bicycle like all my friends in the neighborhood. I was tired of being laughed at because all I had to ride was an old *girl* bicycle that one of my aunts had given us.

I complained to my parents many times about that embarrassing situation, but we didn't have much money back then. I kept bringing it up anyways, until one day my dad told me, "Listen, you want a new bike?"

I answered, "Oh yes, Dad."

He continued, "Well, here's what we will do. If you gather half of the money it costs, I'll pay for the other half."

My eyes opened wide with excitement. But it didn't last long before doubt crept into my heart. I asked my dad, "What will I do to get money?" After all, I was quite young.

He replied, "You could collect empty pop bottles. You just need to ask neighbors if they have any to give you, take what you collect to the store, and the store will give you money for them."

He must have seen my dilemma. That would be very hard for me to do—I was such a shy young boy. I answered hesitantly, "Uh, yes Dad."

His face lit up with enthusiasm and he continued, "But you know where you can find lots and lots of empty bottles? On the side of the road! People throw them out their car windows when they're finished drinking. The ditches are full of them. You know what? I'll go with you on Saturday morning! And we'll bring your little brother to help you, too. I'll drop you off on the side of the road and then drive a little farther away; you'll collect the bottles and bring them to the car; then I'll go a little farther down the road again, and you'll see that you'll be able to get a lot of bottles in no time!"

My dad was right. Lots of people must have been throwing their empty bottles in the ditch, because that summer we found huge quantities of them. But nothing could ever replace in my memories the warm feeling of having my dad coming with me on the journey to my dream.

DREAMS

Dreams. I wouldn't know how to live without them. Sometimes the days get hard, and loud voices want you to be reasonable, to forget those dreams and get on with the program. But once you've received a dream, you can't just quit. Where do they come from? They are so deep inside of us we can't reach the bottom. Do you think God has dreams? That would make sense, since we were created in His image.

I believe the deepest dreams we have are actually the ones the Lord Himself has planted in our hearts; more than that, they are seeds from His dreams. No wonder He wants to come along with us when He sends us to pursue our dreams. He wouldn't miss that for all the gold in the world. He's fulfilling His dreams through us. The one who sends is always found in the company of those He sent. I believe this is important to remember as we progress in our apostolic journeys. It will always remain a joint venture:

With your help I can advance against a troop; with my God I can scale a wall (2 Sam. 22:30).

THE CHAMPIONS ARE HERE

The last decade of the twentieth century and the beginning of the twenty-first have witnessed a resurgence of dreamers. A significant rearrangement of the intercession and prophetic forces has brought fresh fire to the church. New movements have been birthed, and a new breed of revivalists has risen up, refusing to accept the current state of society, with all its social and moral injustices.

Those champions started on a journey to either confront the systems ruling at the top of the mountains of influence or to infiltrate them; in both cases, displacement of the kingdoms of this world by the kingdom of God has been the goal. But the action of these groups of new revivalists has, for the most part, not been able to be embraced within the traditional wineskins of our local churches. Even the emerging apostolic movement, still young and in a formative period, has been struggling to unfold its wings outside the confined space of comfortable and safe Christianity—a bit like young David was hindered by Saul's armor before Goliath (see 1 Sam. 17:38–39).

However, new developments are on the horizon.

HEAVEN'S HEADQUARTERS

The rising of apostolic centers is coming to change the whole paradigm we have been using. God is moving ahead with the next phase of His plan to see His kingdom come on earth. Apostles, surrounded by apostolic teams, will now have the bases of operations they need to activate and release the saints to impact their cities and regions, touching every sphere of society. These apostolic bases are heaven's headquarters to transform the world we live in.

What we will then see is an alignment principle starting to operate in the body of Christ. Leaders with various gifts and ministries will respond to the Holy Spirit's promptings to take their proper places in the global structure God has for His church. Local congregations will be connected to life-giving apostolic centers, and networks will multiply, but instead of acting independently, they will develop interdependently. Apostles and prophets, linked together and solidly grounded in Jesus, will carry a tremendous authority to order the decrees of God to be enforced on the earth. More than a revival, this will be a kingdom being prepared for the Lord.

PASTORS IN TRANSITION

I'm quite sure a number of pastors who read this book will start to realize their gift and vision are in fact that of an apostle, more than anything else. That is not surprising if we consider that the traditional paradigm basically branded all ordained people as pastors. With the present move of God, we can expect to discover many other gifts hiding under the pastor's label. However, not every pastor with a vision is an apostle, and whether they are in pastoral churches or in apostolic centers, the body absolutely needs godly pastors to keep doing what no other gift does as well as they do.

But for those of you who are discovering you are indeed apostles who have been functioning in pastors' garments, and you would now like to transition from your current church setting to an apostolic center, here's a word of advice. Start by asking the Lord to show you a mature apostle you can align with, one who will be able to confirm your gift and calling and help you through your transition. Then, don't be too quick to break the news to those around you that you are an apostle. Many people still misunderstand the term and what it means. Walk softly with people. Give them one bite at the time, and give them a chance to digest between each bite. It took us two years to transition from a traditional church setting into an apostolic center at Le Chemin. Don't be anxious. Let the Holy Spirit work.

AWAKEN THE HEROES

I want to close this book with an appeal to the heroes around us. I am talking about those people who can accomplish great exploits in battle, those who fight like ten men and can make a hundred flee. When these people appear on the battlefield, they make the enemy tremble and yield the way to them. A whole generation of these champions has arisen, and they are tired of seeing the world in the state it is in. They say, "Give me a horse, a sword, and the King's banner." This book is a trumpet blast for those of you in this generation to gather.

But I also know many champions from the older generation have fought for many years without ceasing. They have stood firm in their corners of the land and received many wounds for the Lord. Today they feel tired from all the hits they've received and from the long nights they've spent in the fields. But still, there is a sacred fire in their hearts that doesn't want to die.

Listen, Mighty Warriors, the Lord still needs you. Arise and take courage; He's calling you. A kingdom still needs to be taken.

Église Le Chemin
An Apostolic Center for the 21st Century

480 Vernon Street
Gatineau, Quebec J9J 3K5
CANADA
(819) 778-2681 Web: www.lechemin.ca/index-e.php
Facebook: www.facebook.com/egliselechemin

HODOS

An Apostolic Network for the 21st Century

480 Vernon Street
Gatineau, Quebec J9J 3K5
CANADA
(819) 778-2681
Web: http://www.hodos.ca/index_e.php